SAVING THE
LOST TRIBE

SAVING THE LOST TRIBE

The Rescue and Redemption of the Ethiopian Jews

ASHER NAIM

A PEEKAMOOSE BOOK
BALLANTINE BOOKS
NEW YORK

A Ballantine Book
Published by The Ballantine Publishing Group
Copyright © 2003 by Asher Naim

www.ballantinebooks.com

Library of Congress Cataloging-in-Publication Data

Naim, Asher.
  Saving the lost tribe : the rescue and redemption of the Ethiopian Jews /
Asher Naim.—1st ed.
    p.   cm.
  1. Jews—Ethiopia—History.   2. Operation Solomon, 1991.
3. Naim, Asher.   4. Diplomats—Israel—Biography.   5. Israel—Foreign
relations—Ethiopia.   6. Ethiopia—Foreign relations—Israel.
7. Israel—Ethnic relations.   I. Title.

DS135.E75 N35 2003
325.5694'089'924063—dc21   2002034466

ISBN 0-345-45081-7

Map by Camerapix, Nairobi

Book design by Joseph Rutt

Manufactured in the United States of America

First Edition: January 2003

10 9 8 7 6 5 4 3 2 1

CONTENTS

Contents

Contents

A NOTE TO THE READER

Falasha means "stranger" in Amharic. The Falashas themselves consider it a derogatory term. They call themselves the Beta Israel—the house of Israel. There are many places in the text, however, where the appellation *Beta Israel* created awkwardness, so, in many cases, we have stuck to the more familiar designation of *Falasha*. We would also like to note that in some cases we have taken liberties, conflating both characters and events to ease the flow of the story.

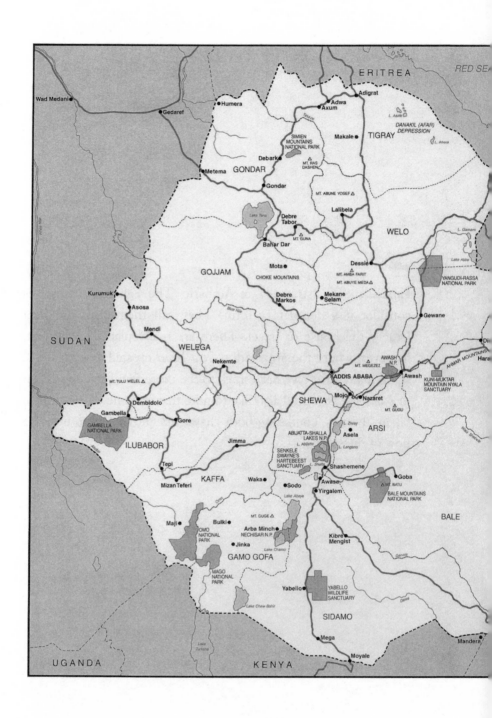

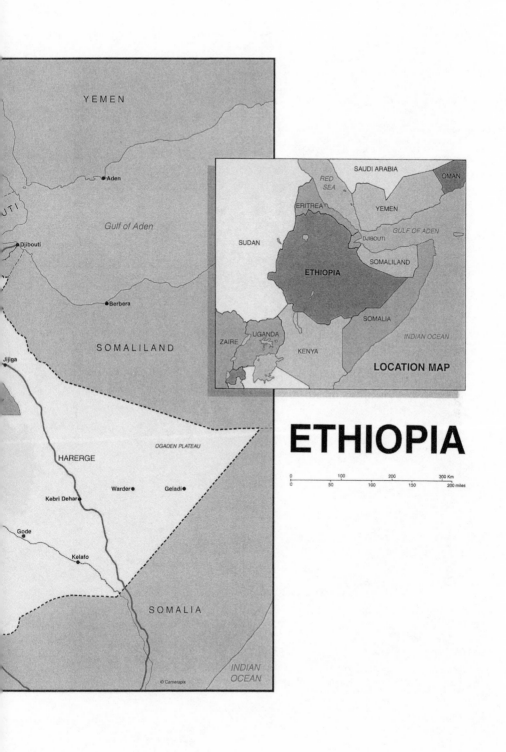

INTRODUCTION

> We are one people, tied to an ancient and splendid faith, and no physical force and no external difference can divide us. For we are one people, there are no black Jews and white Jews: there are Jews. History and Faith bind us together forever.
>
> —*Shimon Peres, former prime minister of Israel*

> Princes shall come out of Egypt, and Ethiopia shall soon stretch her hands to God.
>
> —*Psalms 68:31*

Deep in the rocky terrain of northern Ethiopia, near the spires of the Simian Mountains, a tribe of Jews lived in isolation for hundreds, perhaps thousands of years. They had little or no contact with the outside world. They were agrarians and craftsmen, trading pottery and crude tools with neighboring tribes. For years they struggled to survive against famine and poverty and the marauding armies of their Christian and Muslim neighbors.

In the 1860s, British missionaries traveling through Ethiopia were among the first Westerners to encounter this tribe. When they tried to proselytize, they were shocked to discover that the "burnt faces," as Ethiopians were known to Europeans for their Semitic features and black skin, practiced an ancient form of

Judaism. Tribal members observed Sabbath, maintained strict dietary laws, and performed rituals exactly as they were described in the Hebrew Bible. They even had separate huts, or "red tents," at the edge of their villages for menstruating women and new mothers.

After the missionaries returned to Europe with reports of these black Jews, a Judaic scholar named Joseph Halevy set out to meet them in person. Was it possible these Ethiopians were one of the long-lost tribes of Israel, driven out during the First or Second Temple? With a Muslim guide and a pack of mules, he made the treacherous journey across Ethiopia in the winter of 1867, crossing valleys and rivers and scaling mountains until finally he came across villages of thatched huts.

When Halevy approached, villagers surrounded him. Dressed in pristine white tunics, their children naked and hiding behind them, they were curious but cautious. They had seen a white man only once before when the missionaries came. Halevy greeted them in Amharic, their native tongue, and the tribe buzzed with excitement. He could speak their language! Then the leader of the tribe approached, carrying a bowl of water, possibly for purification purposes; he examined the white man from head to toe.

"Sir," he said, "perhaps you require a knife or sword? You should buy them in a large town. The instruments we make are too rough in workmanship to suit a European. We have nothing here for you, and we don't want to hear about your religion."

"My brethren," Halevy replied. "I don't need a sword. And I'm not here to convert you. I am a European, but like you I am also an Israelite. I worship no god but Adonai, and I acknowledge no other law than the law of Sinai!"

The Ethiopians stared in disbelief. Then slowly laughter rippled through the crowd. Even the leader wore a forgiving smile on his face. "Sir, you a Jew? How can you be a Jew? *You are white!*"

During his first encounter with the Falashas, Halevy had difficulty convincing them he was Jewish. But when he mentioned Jerusalem, as Halevy recounted in his travel journal, the tribe's attitude suddenly "changed as if by magic."

A burning curiosity seemed all at once to have seized the whole company. "Oh, do you come from Jerusalem, the blessed city? Have you beheld with your own eyes Mount Zion, and the House of the Lord of Israel, the Holy Temple? Are you acquainted with the burial place of our mother Rachel?" They eagerly listened to my replies.

The Falashas had been removed from other Jews for thousands of years. None of them had traveled more than a few miles from their village. Yet they had held on to the prospect of one day returning to Jerusalem; it was an idea that burned in their hearts and had been passed down from generation to generation.

More than a century later, I was privileged to play a central part in their redemption, and *Saving the Lost Tribe* is the story of Israel's and America's struggle to reunite the Falashas with the rest of Judaism and deliver them to the Holy Land.

I use the word *redemption* in its ancient sense—a literal "buying back" of the freedom of another person. After the Babylonian exile in 586 BCE, it was considered the responsibility of the tribe to make every effort to buy the freedom of Jewish slaves. This act of redemption, or *lifdod*, was carried out during the Roman Empire and has been made popular today through the heroics of Oskar Schindler, as he is portrayed in *Schindler's List*. No matter what the price, no matter what the risk, it was imperative that every effort was made to redeem the life of another Jew.

Saving the Lost Tribe tells the story of Operation Solomon, the "redemption" of nearly twenty thousand Ethiopian Jews from the clutches of a bloody dictator, which involved months of protracted negotiations and eventually cost thirty-five million dollars (secured by a hundred American donors in less than three days). The operation was a tribute to this original concept of redemption, an inspiration and a reminder of the sacredness of human life that is at the core of Judaism and Western consciousness. We especially need to be reminded of this core value in light of events in the Middle East today.

As much as the Falashas and Operation Solomon are central to *Saving the Lost Tribe,* there is another character in the book that I also became fascinated with and feel compelled to write about—Ethiopia. Images of starving children dying in a desiccated landscape have given the world a false impression of this remarkable country. To understand who the Falashas are and how they remained in total isolation from other Jews and still maintained strict adherence to their faith, one must understand Ethiopia.

Ethiopia is an ancient land, part of the original continent of Gondwanaland. It is the place of our origin as human beings, the land where paleontologists found "Lucy," the near-perfect hominoid skeleton that proved humans were walking upright three million years ago.

Ethiopia has been called the "Tibet of Africa." And like Tibet, its intense and pervasive spirituality is tied inextricably to its physical landscape. Just as Tibet is sequestered behind the formidable wall of the snowy Himalayas, the Ethiopian Plateau, where most of the country's sixty million people live, is protected from its neighbors by geography. The plateau, more than six thousand feet in elevation, rises out of the African continent in splendid isolation, protected on the north and east by the Red Sea and fearsome deserts of sulfur and tar where the temperature tops 130 degrees Fahrenheit. To the west are deep, impassable gorges and dense jungle; to the south, a seemingly endless expanse of barren, baked scrubland.

The plateau is home to a landscape that rivals the drama of Tibet. The thirteen-thousand-foot peaks of the massive Simian and Tigray Mountain ranges tower over the uplands. Crystal-clear trout streams tumble from their cloud-shrouded slopes into large lakes where huge flocks of flamingos roost and hippos bask in the shallows. Lush eucalyptus groves open onto pristine prairies dotted with herds of zebra, antelope, and gazelle. Muscular, serpentine rivers wind through spectacular gorges; in their lower elevations these rivers are home to fearsome Nile crocodiles, which can grow more than thirty feet in length. Ethiopia is home to 85 percent of the Nile's water, and the source of the Blue Nile is Ethiopia's Lake Tana. This is the country that was called the Land of the Gods by the ancient Egyptians, and it is on this central plateau that the remarkable civilization that Ethiopia produced was born and flourished.

As a result of its isolation, Ethiopia is the only African country with a distinct language, and the only African state that was never colonized by a Western power, except for a short Italian conquest (1935–1941). And like Tibet it is rich in its own singular spiritual heritage. It is the only African country dominated by the Bible. More than 50 percent of the Ethiopians are Christian. They preserve and maintain one of the oldest forms of Christianity in the world, which took hold in Ethiopia in the fourth century.

Ethiopians, both Jews and Christians, trace their heritage back to Menelik I, who claimed to be descended from King Solomon and the Queen of Sheba. Sheba, the legend goes, was an Ethiopian queen. The emperors of Ethiopia, including the last emperor, Haile-Selassie, who died in 1974, claimed to be the direct descendants of the apocryphal union between Solomon and Sheba.

As you'll see, I was, at first, a reluctant actor in the saga of the Falashas. But the time I have spent with them has been the richest and most meaningful in my diplomatic career of thirty years. I offer this story to you, of a little-known but profoundly moving people and a mysterious and ancient land.

Jerusalem, August 2002

PART ONE

A DROP OF BLOOD

BUBOT

November 11, 1990

T he Peugeot 504 barreled through the pitted streets of Addis Ababa, the capital of Ethiopia, a blue-and-white Israeli flag flapping on its hood. I leaned into its plush backseat. Next to me was Uri Lubrani, a high-level Israeli official in the Ministry of Defense who had gotten me into this mess. The Peugeot plunged into a pothole, suspension rocking, and Lubrani shot me a doleful glance. Lubrani always looks like he's expecting the worst. I paid no attention. I had just arrived in Addis and would soon be meeting with President Mengistu Haile Miriam. Perhaps he was ready to permit the thousands of Beta Israel, the black Ethiopian Jews encamped in Addis, to emigrate to Israel. As the newly appointed Israeli ambassador, I had to conduct the hair-trigger negotiations for their release.

It was not a job I had wanted. I had just concluded a two-year ambassadorship in Finland, orchestrating the emigration of tens of thousands of Russian Jews from what was then the Soviet

Union to Israel. I'd barely unpacked in my home in Jerusalem when I'd been reassigned. As a professional diplomat I'm accustomed to a whir of time zones, countries, and cultures. But I needed a break, and I'd been pushed into service yet again.

I wondered, fleetingly, why Lubrani had refused the ambassadorship. He loved the limelight. Saving Jews was always a popular cause with the higher-ups with whom Lubrani loved to consort. Perhaps he'd declined because the risk of failure was high. Instead, he had chosen to oversee the operation, a role that would send him to Washington, his destination of choice. If the mission succeeded, he would hog the credit; if it failed, it would be my bones that would be broken into a million pieces, as we say in Hebrew—but not, God willing, in the way that had almost happened to my predecessor.

The Peugeot was almost brand-new, used for only six months by the last Israeli ambassador, Meir Yoffe. A Libyan operative (a terrorist with a diplomatic passport) had placed a briefcase bomb in the stall of a public bathroom in the Hilton where Yoffe was using the facilities. Fortunately the Libyans, as usual, botched the operation. The bomb exploded but Yoffe escaped unscathed. He always used the stall they booby-trapped, but for some reason he had changed stalls that day, and it had saved his life. His nerves, however, were shot; he'd had enough of Ethiopia.

I rode through Addis, past peeling billboards of Mengistu and Lenin. The road was a mess. Mengistu had poured Ethiopia's resources into his army, the largest in Africa, and left the rest of the country to rot. Addis itself was a typical sub-Saharan African city—a huge village of huts, mud houses, shanties, and an occasional building. Soldiers in uniform picked their way through emaciated beggars, flies clustered around their lips and eyes. Barefoot women in long brightly colored robes walked with a swaying gait, baskets on their heads. Cars and scooters flew like bats out of hell, weaving around the donkeys, cattle, and sheep that roamed the streets.

"Run over a sheep, sir, and you must pay a hundred birr," said my driver Konata, a man to whom I'd taken an immediate liking. "The courts are full."

"Of dead sheep?"

"Yes, sir! But a pregnant sheep is 150 birr"—about twenty-five dollars.

"*Nu?*"

"So now every sheep is pregnant!"

We shared a laugh: Africa in a nutshell. I knew this because I was born and raised in Tripoli, and in the 1960s I had directed Israel's aid program in Africa. At that time I had been a great Africa enthusiast. We in Israel were convinced that Africa was the continent of the future. So rich in resources! So much promise! We saw the African independence movements of the 1960s as an immensely positive sign. They had cast off colonial shackles and forged national identities, just as we Jews had done in 1948. But by the time I came to Addis, like so many others, I was deeply disappointed. Corruption, greed, and selfishness had plagued Africa. On the surface (although I was to learn that this appearance was deceptive), Ethiopia was typical—rebels, poverty, famine, dictatorship, and disease.

WE WENT STRAIGHT to the ambassador's residence—a suite at the Hilton. A round-the-clock guard of Ethiopian soldiers had been posted outside my door. The government didn't want the Libyans pulling another Yoffe.

"Get rid of the *bubot*," said David, my chief of security. *Bubot* are dolls who do nothing.

David was in his late twenties, balding on top, wide as a door and silent on his feet. He carried a black Beretta strapped on his back just above the belt. We had plenty of weapons in Addis—Uzis hidden in a safe house and at the embassy. I had been trained in small arms before I came, a refresher course, really, since I had fought in the army and served in the reserves.

"No, no," I said. "I don't want to hurt their feelings."

"Feelings! What do their feelings have to do with your safety?"

This was fast becoming a typical Israeli argument. David's Hebrew had heated up and the Ethiopian guards were wide-eyed. What would have happened to them if they had rebuked a superior in such a tone? They had no idea what was coming next.

I laid my hand on David's arm and took him aside. "Just their presence will serve as deterrent. Don't argue with me on this."

He shook his head, unrepentant, and it wasn't long before I displeased him again. Yoffe's suite had been on the seventh floor, but I didn't want to rely on the elevator every time I wanted to go in or out. David fumed. I was too accessible, he argued. I overruled him.

I could see David was containing himself. He put his own security team of two men in place, members of our specially trained secret service. David wanted me to keep a pistol in my suite, but I said no. If there was a gun around, there was a chance that I'd use it. That was David's job, and I put my faith in him. All security people are a nudge. Wherever I go, I always sign a paper relieving them of responsibility if I'm blown up or shot. Then I do what I want.

My suite on the lower floor was comfortable—two bedrooms, two baths, sitting room, and kitchenette. In the midst of all the chaos, the Hilton was still a Hilton. My balcony looked out over the ten-foot-high wall that enclosed the hotel's grounds against the jumble of the city. Big mountains, green up their slopes, rose into the African sunset.

Darkness fell, and I went out on the lawns that stretched away into shadows of the flowering trees. David was at my side. The city murmured beyond the high walls. Empty tennis courts were lit up under blazing lights. No one swam in the heated pool; the smell of chlorine rose off its unruffled surface. Most foreigners had already jumped ship. The staff stood around doing nothing. I ordered a soda from one of the servers. A scooter backfired as she brought it and she cringed, the bottle dropping to the grass. She retrieved it with a graceful curtsy and long, slender fingers.

I watched how she startled at the slightest sound. Who would be rounded up, tortured, and shot by the army tonight? Who would be caught violating the citywide curfew? Guards in army uniforms, cradling rifles, were posted at the hotel gates. Their eyes slid over us toward the dark hills where defeat drew daily closer. Death squads, war, famine—interminable carnage. The wider world went on, oblivious to the misery and terror. But I could smell the fear.

CHUPPALOGIA

A month earlier, on October 11, the phone had rung in my home in Jerusalem. My wife, Hilda, and I were unpacking, glad to be back from Finland. I had spent three years of duty as minister in the Israeli embassy in Washington, D.C., then two years as ambassador to Finland, and so I was relieved to get back to Israel for a much-needed break from my travels.

Director General Reuven Merhav of the Foreign Ministry was calling to insist that I come to the ministry for an immediate briefing on Ethiopia.

"I'm in my boxer shorts!" I told him, annoyed. "We've just returned."

"All right." He sounded exhausted. "I'll send Uri Lubrani to you."

Now I knew he meant business. The Foreign Ministry only borrowed Lubrani from the Ministry of Defense for high-level affairs.

"Ethiopia," Hilda said when she heard what was happening. "What do you know about Ethiopia? Tell them to get another man."

"I know! I know! We'll give them lunch and send them packing."

The doorbell rang promptly at noon.

"Asher!" Lubrani greeted me, one old warrior to another, a shock of unruly black hair drooping down over his forehead. "Meet Haim Divon."

Divon, in his forties, with his baby face, was a simpatico type—always smiling, good natured, and able. I knew him from around the ministry. He'd been our man in Colombo, not ambassador exactly because Sri Lanka doesn't have full diplomatic relations with Israel. Call him a "representative."

Hilda set out plates of hummus, tomatoes, olives, and pita. "Look, Uri," I said. "What is this about Ethiopia?"

The playfully belligerent tone my countrymen take with each other evaporated. "Asher, something important has come up."

Through the 1980s, Lubrani had been in charge of the affairs in dealing with Lebanon—which meant he could stomach anything. I felt the weight of his eyes on me, the heaviness of all those years in Lebanon, the thanklessness of it.

"I'm listening."

"You remember Operation Moses?"

"Vaguely."

"It was carried out by Mossad with CIA help from 1982 to 1984. Thousands of Falashas walked four hundred miles from Ethiopia into Sudan. The operation was a secret because our Muslim friends in Sudan did not want to be seen helping Jews."

"I remember. People claiming to be Jews were showing up in UN Red Cross refugee camps."

"Some fourteen thousand Falashas attempted the exodus," said

Lubrani. "About eight thousand made it. The rest died on the journey or were turned back or arrested by Mengistu's troops. Then, because of media coverage of the event in June 1984, the operation ceased. Tens of thousands of Falashas were left stranded in Ethiopia. Mengistu severed relations with us and ceased all emigration of black Jews."

Divon had stopped smiling. He took up the thread. "This impasse would have continued, but then Mengistu's arms supplier, the Soviet Union, went belly-up. Arab countries turned against him and began aiding the rebels. He was losing his civil war. Guess what? He decided to come to Tel Aviv a year ago June."

"I had no idea," I said.

"No one knew!" Lubrani popped an olive in his mouth.

"Mengistu wanted arms in exchange for releasing the Falashas," said Divon. "Shamir didn't say yes, he didn't say no; he bought time. Mengistu reestablished diplomatic relations. Yoffe went to Addis. Mengistu allowed a few hundred Falashas to rejoin their families who were already in Israel. Then came the bathroom bombing. Yoffe left. Mengistu awaits his replacement."

Lubrani broke in: "Listen, Asher. It hasn't been easy to find the right person. Mengistu wants a top man. Someone senior with influence and experience."

Hilda scoffed, but I was not immune to this kind of flattery.

"Hilda, please," he said. Now I knew what a strain he must be under. He's impossible to ruffle; he'd doze through an air raid. "The time Shamir bought is running out," he continued. "Rebels defeat Mengistu at every turn. They won't talk to us because they think we've sided with him! And a woman named Susan Pollack of the American Association for Ethiopian Jews has induced thousands of Falashas to abandon their homes in the north and come to our embassy in Addis. The American Jews hoped that would force us to act quickly to bring the Falashas to Israel. Mengistu sees an opportunity. He's ready to deal. We have to get these Falashas out, but we can't give Mengistu what he wants. I won't kid you, Asher. It's going to be tricky. We don't even want to think what would happen if Mengistu decides you've been stringing him along!"

I glanced at Hilda, but she didn't bat an eye. I met my wife when she came to Jerusalem in 1954, one of the few Americans in Israel at the time, on a scholarship to Hebrew University where I was studying law. We Israeli boys used to joke that American Jewish girls came here to study chuppalogia. I liked her instantly— what was inside was outside. Nothing was hidden. I married her without meeting her family. I had my suitcase and she had hers. We started from zero. I was the son of a barber. She came from a family of modest means. She knew what it was to marry an Israeli and come here to live. It hasn't always been easy.

"We know what happened to Yoffe," she said in her easy Hebrew with its Boston vowels. From the look on her face, I could see her concern. But I also knew she would want me to go.

I turned to Lubrani. "You want me to go like Moses to this dictator and say, in so many words, 'Let my people go!' But what happens if God doesn't come down to help me out with miracles and plagues?"

"*Nu*," said Lubrani. "If God doesn't appear we have the next best thing."

"And what's that?"

"The Americans!"

Even Hilda had to laugh.

THE HYENA FEEDERS

Absolutism tempered by assassination.

—Count Munster

A month later, there I was in the back of the Peugeot, with Lubrani by my side, preparing to meet Mengistu. I wasn't sure what to expect. Mengistu was called the Butcher of Addis, a man who reportedly rose to power by killing Emperor Haile-Selassie in the back of a limousine with his bare hands. Since his reign began, his army or his oppressive rule had killed more than one million Ethiopians. That was the reason why he was also called the Black Stalin of Africa.

We pulled up to a crossing guard at the presidential palace. There was a neat guardhouse and soldiers dressed in crisp green khaki jackets, green pants, high black boots, and khaki military caps drawn forward, members of Mengistu's special unit—ten thousand troops under his personal command. They didn't bother to check our papers; we were expected. A paved drive curved through groomed grounds to wide marble steps that led into a modern one-story building, freshly painted white. This was where Mengistu worked, but nobody knew where he slept. Sources said he lived a simple life, which indicated the complexity of his character.

It was odd, but I was looking forward to this meeting. Call it morbid curiosity: I had met with many world leaders but no one of quite this caliber of evil. I wanted to take measure of the man, to look for weakness, to see how I would stand against him.

Mrs. Sheune, personal head of protocol, a plump stern woman, waddled quickly toward us. "Come, come," she said in fluent English. "You are expected!" We signed the visiting book and cooled our heels. Mrs. Sheune bustled about. Posters of the dazzling Ethiopian countryside and a smiling Mengistu looked down on us from the walls.

Mrs. Sheune picked up the phone and slammed it down. "Come!" she ordered. Her stoutness parted the air before us. We were sucked along in her wake; her square heels made a sharp clippity-clop on the marble floor.

A DIPLOMAT'S FACE is his place of business, and I put on a genteel and affable expression as we went in to see Mengistu. I knew very little about his origins. Information was scarce. He had grown up in Addis, where his mother was a servant to descendants of the imperial household. He was probably the illegitimate son to the head of this household, Master Kabede, the uncle of Mengistu's closest adviser, Kasa Kabede. That would explain why his mother's employer had paid for his military education.

Mengistu was standing when Mrs. Sheune closed the door behind us, and he came forward to greet us. He was a short man, thin, in his forties, neatly dressed in a light blue suit. Over a full sensitive mouth he had a thin mustache trimmed very close. His cheeks were smooth. Behind wire-rimmed spectacles his eyes had a searching quality. He wore military boots of hard, unbending leather. It struck me that he had been in uniform and had quickly changed into a jacket and tie for this meeting. How could this rather unassuming, sensitive-looking man be a bloody tyrant? Looking at him it didn't make sense. But then Hitler and Stalin could be unassuming.

Mengistu was obviously pleased to see us. He smiled warmly (which I was to learn was a rare event). I sensed his isolation. The rebels were closing in, his country was bankrupt, the Soviets, history. No one came to see him, so we were a big deal. For a moment I almost felt sorry for him. I had to remind myself who he was.

The room was large, a hall really, empty but for a long couch against the wall and three armchairs. We were briefly introduced to the foreign minister, a nondescript middle-aged man in a cheap blue suit who, during the meeting, sat in stony silence at a remove from us. Mengistu did not offer us food or drink. Girma, a man in his midfifties with only one arm, translated our English into Amharic, an ancient Semitic language that bears some relationship to both Hebrew and Arabic. This gave Mengistu time to compose his replies, which he gave in Amharic. It was an irksome process—especially since it was clear Mengistu's English was fluent. He'd had several tours of the United States when he was in the army and occasionally corrected the translator, who was clearly terrified of making too many mistakes.

Mengistu pointed us to the chairs and then sat himself down on the couch. The meeting began well. Lubrani immediately played our trump card. He confirmed that, at Mengistu's request, he had spoken to the State Department and President George Bush had appointed a special envoy to come from the United States to Ethiopia to meet with the dictator (this meeting had been Merhav's idea). Mengistu was clearly excited by the prospect of this tripartite meeting: He leaned forward and his eyes lit up. He hoped to persuade the Americans to ante up arms and aid. As long as he thought we could influence the Americans, he would try to please us. Lubrani also reminded him that we had come across with an aid package to train health workers as well as teaching advanced agriculture and animal husbandry, and I had come, a veteran diplomat, to take Yoffe's place.

It was my turn. I spoke in English. "I'm happy to be here. Our countries have had long history of friendship. I'm not an Ethiopian scholar, but I'll try to learn."

Mengistu said he was pleased that I had come and looked forward to a meeting with the U.S. representative. He added that he would arrange for me to tour Ethiopia to get to know the country.

"Thank you," I answered. "I'd very much like to see where the Falashas came from." I mentioned the main reason for my presence carefully. "The recognition of the Falashas as Jews is a hugely important step in Israel's maturation. And our Ethiopians want their relatives to join them in Israel."

Mengistu raised his hand to stop me. "There was no problem with unification of families before Operation Moses. All the Falashas were in their homes in the hills of Ethiopia. Now, you say that unless we allow them to 'rejoin' their relatives in Israel, we have done the world a grave injustice. But it was only through the Jewish Agency that they left the highlands in the first place and came to the idea that they were exiles deserving of return. I must be frank with you. I have worked for the good of Ethiopia my whole life. I know this country like the back of my hand. If you start picking out Jews from the non-Jews, you will have all of Ethiopia in Israel. Why? Because we were all Jews before we adopted Christianity in the fourth century. So where do you draw the line? It is a hornets' nest, as I think you will find . . ."

I had heard this theory—that Ethiopia was Jewish before it became Christian; but I thought it was just that, a theory. I had no idea at the time how prophetic Mengistu's words would turn out to be. I had to bite my tongue. Mengistu's talk of knowing Ethiopia and working for its people made me want to get up and walk out. He was a killer and he was holding Jews hostage for weapons to keep his bloody regime afloat.

"Arrange for the ambassador to go anywhere he wishes," Mengistu said to his foreign minister. Thank goodness my response hadn't registered in my expression. At that moment I realized the tenuousness of my position. Mengistu made nice because he thought that he was going to get something from us. But neither we nor the Americans were going to give him what he wanted—and then the honeymoon would be over.

I thought we were done, but the meeting dragged on for three hours as Mengistu reviewed the history of the conflict with the rebels, the Somalian invasion of Ethiopia in 1977, and the duplicity of his former Soviet allies. We knew all of it already, and by the time it was over I felt bludgeoned, consumed by a rubbery numbness and an overwhelming urge to empty my bladder.

At last, we stood. A shiver of distaste prickled my nape as I grasped his hand. The searching eyes. The sensitive mouth. The thin mustache. I made a beeline for the bathroom, and took some deep breaths as Mrs. Sheune hustled us out of the building to our waiting car. Konata held the door. Relief was plain on his face—either that we were leaving the domain of the dragon or that I had emerged intact. Probably a bit of both.

We were both fed up. "He's a stupid man," I said of Mengistu. "How did he come to power?"

"Fast on the draw," said Lubrani. "He killed everyone who was in his way."

AT THAT MOMENT, a man of medium height, with a bulging belly and powerful shoulders, came forward with an incandescent smile and an outstretched hand.

"May I present Kasa Kabede," said Lubrani. "A man with two portfolios—head of the Cadre and foreign policy. Most important, he is Mengistu's main adviser on relations with the United States and Israel. He is the one you'll be dealing with on questions of Falasha emigration."

"Shalom," said Kasa. "I have heard about your exploits in Washington, and I'm looking forward to working together."

I was shocked: His Hebrew was fluent. "Where did you learn Hebrew?" I asked.

"I went to Hebrew University from 1960 to 1965."

Lubrani whispered in my ear: "He was called the Prince of Ethiopia, the Black Stallion of Africa, when he was at the university for his reputation with the ladies."

"I can see why," I said. The man was very polished; he exuded vitality and charm.

"I'd like to have you over to the house for dinner. To get to know each other," he said before we parted.

"That would be delightful," I replied.

"Watch him," said Lubrani as we exited the palace. "He is as cunning as he is charming. Truly, in him you will have met your match."

"How did he come to study at Hebrew University?"

"It's quite interesting," said Lubrani. "Kasa's father accompanied Haile-Selassie when he came to Jerusalem for four months before going to England, after Mussolini invaded Ethiopia in 1935."

"I had no idea Haile-Selassie was in Jerusalem."

"He lived in the Rahavia neighborhood and would walk the streets each afternoon with an aide holding a colorful umbrella over his head and an entourage of five officials walking behind him. I've heard he walked slowly with a perpetually sad expression. When the emperor left for London, Kabede stayed in Jerusalem and mixed with the Jewish community. He was particularly impressed with Hebrew University. When Kasa came of age he sent him to study there. Kasa had a grand time. He belonged to a Bohemian group of artists, writers, and intellectuals. But then he became too seriously involved with an Israeli woman. His father brought him home to marry an Ethiopian."

"I can see that's it both an advantage and disadvantage that he's so familiar with Israel."

"Yes," sighed Lubrani. "Sometimes I feel he knows us better than we know ourselves."

LUBRANI WENT BACK to the hotel. David was waiting for me in the Peugeot. "I want to show you something, Asher," he said. "I want you to see something that diplomats don't see."

"Please, sirs, where?" Konata asked.

David gave Konata instructions. The crossing guard rose. Konata stomped on the accelerator and the Peugeot pivoted into the traffic. Wind rushed in through the open windows. The car banked, and gravel kicked up under the wheels as we swung around. We raced through the dust, children throwing up their hands, jumping up and down and screaming at the sight of white men in a fancy car. Small fires burned by the road. Livestock scattered before us. Monkeys loped through the treetops and scampered along the ragged crests of the city's ubiquitous walls. Hovels and huts opened onto green plains. We shot past women carrying straw baskets on their heads filled with stones. Their bare feet seemed one with the red dirt paths that ran like shallow canals by the roadside; their necks were slim and strong.

"Why are they carrying stones?" I asked Konata.

"To build the walls, sir," he said.

"But there are plenty of stones all over the place. Why do they need to carry them on their heads?"

Konata shrugged.

We entered a dusty hinterland of huts and shacks, fallow fields, dense patches of forest. Some of the shacks had a tall wooden pole in front, topped with an empty can.

"What are those poles?" I asked Konata.

"Bars, sir. One-stool bars. Only one man may come. They are managed by the woman of the house. She gives him something to eat and drink."

"And what else?" said David. "Tell him about the curtain, Konata."

Konata stared straight ahead. "Oh, sir, it is a great shame about the curtain. If it is opened to the bed the man knows he can lie with her or maybe one of her daughters. It is sad, sir. We are a very poor people."

"Before you start getting any ideas, Ambassador," said David, "this road is used by truck drivers. The AIDS rate is high, and, of course, the disease is spreading through the country."

David leaned forward and said something to Konata, who pushed the Peugeot even harder. We topped eighty miles an hour, which on these roads was no joke. Konata drove like a man possessed.

"We have to hurry to be back before curfew," said David.

Terraced fields dropped into green valleys. We traveled east, past groups of people with donkeys loaded down with burlap sacks and huge sheaves of *teff*, the tiny round grain used for making *injera*, the pancakelike bread that was served with every meal.

Konata stopped the car and we stood at a clearing's edge. No houses were in sight, but the air was rich with the smell of wood smoke and burning dung. We were not alone.

"Sirs, when they come you give them a few birr, okay?"

Three men, who had been squatting around a fire at the clearing's center, rose. I thought they carried shepherd's staffs but as they approached I saw these were spears. Dressed in rags, they had small sacks slung across their shoulders. Their arms and cheeks were marked with diagonal slashes—self-inflicted scars.

"*Haradim*, sirs," said Konata softly. "Before many people came to watch them. Lots of tourists. But now, with the war, no one comes."

One hundred birr is what I gave the eldest. They turned without a word and we followed them toward the clearing's edge. The trees were a black parapet against the dusk. It was cool now. The air was fresh, the wind coming down from the mountains. I felt Africa in my bones. Somewhere I heard the sound of water against stone. The earth seemed to breathe, and the grass rasped against the fabric of my slacks. The headman extended his thin arm downward, made a shallow inverted cup with his hand, and held it above the restless grass. We stopped just short of the trees, the *haradim* standing in a neat line, their spears rising through the cradle of their arms.

"Meat!" David whispered as the men reached into their sacks.

"Hehehehehehe!" they suddenly cried, a mad cackle that sent birds rocketing from the trees. From the forest's edge we watched humped shapes emerge, sidling slowly, wary but drawn irresistibly forward.

"Hyenas!" hissed Konata, and I could see them now, magnificently ugly, their tawny coats patched with black, rough as door-mats, yellow eyes, and the stink of them, a smell of rotting flesh. Their faces looked like enormous bats, some monstrous hybrid of feline and canine, half snarling, half pleading, salivating as the men held out their hands and the hyenas stretched out their necks, front legs planted far forward, back legs cocked, and took the meat in a gentle, almost licking motion from the *haradim*'s fingers. The hyenas wolfed down the meat with sharp gagging intakes of breath and a wet clenching of their huge jaws.

I had seen enough. I turned around to go back to the car, David following close behind.

"Sometimes, Asher," David said, "they take more than meat. They take the whole arm. Do you know why I brought you to *haradim*?"

I stopped and turned around to face him. "No I don't."

He gripped my arm. "With Mengistu you may think you have tamed him. He will eat from your hand, take what you give. But in one second he can turn and strike. Then you have no more hand. No more arm. And it's the same thing with this country. I have heard about your reputation. That you like to do things your own way. But please remember Yoffe. Please remember that you are in danger here."

We drove through the gathering dusk. Soon it was night and we raced along. The soldiers who imposed the 9:00 P.M. curfew had no watches. They had been known to shoot first and then ask for the time.

At the hotel, I took the stairs to my suite, shed my clothes, and took a long hot shower until the stench of carrion was gone. In the kitchenette, I made myself a sandwich, standing out on the balcony to eat it. The city dimly flickered. My people were out there; I wanted to be among them. Next to this, Helsinki was heaven. For centuries, the Beta Israel had thought they were the last Jews on earth. They were a lost tribe, tucked away in the mountains of the north. Now they were poised on the brink of annihilation. I felt a tremendous weight upon me. I heard the wet clenching of the hyenas' jaws. Who were these people? It was quiet. The curfew had come. Now only the army and its informers were moving on the streets.

FOUR

FIVE HUNDRED BIRR

God doesn't want us to do extraordinary things;
he wants us to do ordinary things extraordinarily
well.

—*Bernard S. Raskas*

I stood on the same balcony the next morning, watching Konata polish the Peugeot. It was parked on the grass beneath my window. In this poor country, the car was worth a king's ransom.

The rainy season had just ended: The air was cool and clean. On the street past the hotel's back gate, I could see many people walking with vigor and purpose. There was no lassitude; little apathy. Ethiopia's poverty hadn't killed its vitality.

The Hilton was across the boulevard from the Ethiopian Foreign Ministry, a four-story concrete building painted light green. I would be able to walk to where I would conduct most of my business. The ministry abutted the grounds of the imperial palace where Haile-Selassie, the last in Ethiopia's long line of emperors, had ruled.

Haile-Selassie still casts a long shadow over Ethiopia, indeed over much of Africa. The world's last absolute monarch, he was heir to a dynastic line that had ruled Ethiopia from 1270 to 1973. He was the author of pan-Africanism and African nationalism—a symbol of nascent African independence and the spiritual leader of the worldwide Rastafarian movement. Which was why African leaders had chosen Addis as the center of the Organization of African Unity (OAU).

In his latter years, Selassie became deeply eccentric, perhaps senile. He was a complete introvert, rising at 4:00 A.M. to attend mass in his private chapel, wandering the hallways of the imperial palace at night, seemingly indifferent to the waves of famine that gripped his country. No decision of importance could be made by his ministers without his approval. It was a devastating way to run as complicated a country as Ethiopia. Karl Marx said that each sociopolitical structure carries within itself the seeds of its destruction—so it was with Ethiopia's imperial dynasty.

Although he was a deeply flawed ruler, Haile-Selassie is remembered for the moral challenge he put to the world. In 1935, Mussolini invaded Ethiopia and massacred thousands of Ethiopian civilians. Ethiopia was then the only African state that was a member of the League of Nations. Haile-Selassie appealed to them—in vain.

KONATA WORKED THE chamois over the car's black finish. Birds flitted in the foliage. Just down the block I could make out an iron bust of Lenin, four stories tall—a gift from North Korea. The bust was offered as comradely gesture from one despotic regime to another. Ethiopians joked that Lenin faced the airport, which signified that he was on the way out.

I reentered my suite. Adanich, my maid, had prepared breakfast: fresh orange juice, rye toast, delicious Ethiopian coffee, and strawberry jam. She was wrapped in silence and sorrow. Her rail-thin body was covered by a brown smock that fell below her knees. She wore shabby shoes without socks. Her dark eyes were very big in her long face. Her permanently sad look changed when I spoke to her; she always turned to me smiling, and her beauty came out. Like many Ethiopians (who had studied it in school), she spoke some English. As Adanich served breakfast, I asked about her family.

"They took them to the army," she said of her three brothers.

"Who?"

"Soldiers at night. They beat my brothers and took them away."

Here she fell silent. I waited for more as she washed my dishes and I dried, over her protests and much to her amazement (Hilda has me well trained).

"And?" I prompted.

"Three months after we had a letter. Tesfaye died fighting. He is buried far away in Tigray country."

"And your second brother?"

"He came home with no leg." Here she paused. "My third brother ran from the army. Now he is in hiding and will be shot if they catch him. He wants to go to Kenya. Mama is afraid." This she said in a low voice, not meeting my eyes. "We need five hundred birr for travel and, when he crosses the border, paying the *shifta*"—bandits. Then she looked at me as to say, Will you give us the five hundred birr to save my brother?

I ignored her question. My position made it impossible for me to be a party to an illegal act. I live by the saying, however, that to handle yourself, use your head; to handle others, use your heart. At the end of the month, I doubled Adanich's salary, because, I said, she was so wonderful at her job. She beamed with gratitude. When she tried to thank me on behalf of her family, I turned away as if I hadn't heard her. A few weeks later, she told me that her brother was "alive," meaning his escape had succeeded.

FIVE

THE FORBEARANCE OF JOB

Only a life lived for others is a life worthwhile.
— *Albert Einstein*

K onata looked up at the window of my suite and waited for Adanich to signal him that I was coming down. As soon as I appeared, he stopped his polishing and opened the car's back door, shutting it behind me. He ran around the car, hopped into the driver's seat, and looked expectantly at me in the rearview mirror.

"Where to, sir?"

"The embassy."

Konata gravely nodded his head, and the car smoothly accelerated, turning eastward out of the Hilton's back gate. The gatekeeper in his green uniform several sizes too large for his spindly body saluted with a toothless grin. Which wasn't the norm. Most people in Ethiopia, from what I had seen, had excellent teeth.

The city's streets were lined with pedestrians and their animals moving in an endless ragged stream in both directions. This would be my first visit to the embassy. I had no idea what to expect. We drove for about twenty minutes over mostly unpaved roads—a conspicuous presence in the new black car. New cars were a rarity in Addis and almost, I would learn, nonexistent in the rest of the country. Only high government officials had cars like the Peugeot. The small middle class made do with wrecks.

Donkeys swayed under loads of *teff*, mangos, bananas, papayas, avocados, apples, pears, tomatoes, cucumbers, green peppers, lots of red-hot peppers (a staple in Ethiopian cooking), watermelon, and sugarcane, which people peeled and ate raw. The produce was paltry and worm-eaten.

The trucks made an enormous racket and traveled at a snail's pace. Many of them came from the port of Assab on the Red Sea and carried merchandise to the Mercato, Addis's central market, perhaps the largest in Africa. In the Mercato, the Ethiopian saying goes, one can buy anything except a man's soul. From the coast to Addis is only three hundred miles, but the trip typically took two days. Two nights on the road with a bar woman who supplied the truck driver with everything he needed—food, drink, a place to sleep, and sex.

Most of the faces on the street looked as though the happiness had been leached out of them. They spread their wares on old sacks on the dusty earth. An old woman sold empty Coca-Cola cans, used plastic bags, a battered shoeshine brush, yellowed newspapers, pencils, a pair of socks.

Konata turned onto a gravel road that led up a small hill to the large wooded compound of the Israeli embassy. Near the embassy building, hundreds of Ethiopians milled about, stood on lines, waited in groups to be served by two dozen *shlichim* (agents) from the Jewish Agency and the Joint Distribution Committee (JDC), an American organization that helps Jews in need all over the world. The JDC financed all the expenses for upkeep, medical support, and feeding of the Beta Israel while they were in Addis. This cost ran into the millions of dollars.

The embassy was in shambles. Israel had closed it following the suspension of the diplomatic relations with Ethiopia after our 1973 war with the Arabs and leased it to the Swedish Aid Office. They had let it fall into near ruin. Its concrete facade was crumbling; its gardens were weed infested.

"Shalom!" Amir Maimon, my assistant, greeted me. He was twenty-eight, slim, from a Yemenite family, his skin dark, his features fine. I had been acquainted with his father, a general in the Israeli Defense Forces (IDF). Maimon himself had been a captain in the IDF, resigned his commission, and passed the Foreign Ministry entrance exam. This is no small feat: Typically, a thousand applicants compete for twenty vacancies to apprentice with diplomats. Addis was Maimon's first assignment abroad.

"Nice of you to arrange for all these people to greet me," I said as we entered the embassy. "You did this to impress me?"

People lined steps, sat in hallways, huddled on the floors. *Shlichim* worked in the corridors on narrow tables and in the crowded rooms, registering new arrivals and issuing their ID cards: four-by-six-inch pieces of paper that contained basic data: name, date, place of birth, date of arrival in Addis, marital status, number of children, and a photograph of the cardholder. Heads of households had IDs.

My second-floor office had a small outer room where Yengus, my Ethiopian secretary, worked. She stood as I entered, a woman in Western dress about thirty years old, black hair combed neatly to the side. She made a little bow and then stared at the floor in stony silence. I tried to engage her in conversation but failed. She bowed again and sat at her desk with its typewriter and two telephones. To her left was a small table with a fax machine.

My room was to the right. It was fairly large. At one time its parquet wood floor must have been beautiful. But now it was scuffed, the dirt worn into its battered surface. The room was sparsely furnished—an old table with two wooden chairs, no pictures on the walls, and an electric heater in the corner. There was dust on the telephones. The room was a stark contrast to my office in Helsinki with its plush carpet, flowers, and Swedish furniture. But one thing the Addis office did have in its favor was its perch: a wide window overlooked the compound. I would be able to see everything that was going on.

IN THE MAIN lobby, I was greeted by Zimna Berhane, an Ethiopian *shaliach*, a short man, wide in the shoulders, balding, with glasses, fluent Hebrew, and a happy face. He seemed to revel in the atmosphere of barely contained chaos. The scene at the embassy was the culmination of his life's work—pushing for the recognition of Ethiopian Jews and their repatriation to Israel. He was one of the first twelve teenagers brought by the Jewish Agency to Israel in 1955 to train as teachers and return to Falasha villages in Ethiopia to teach Hebrew, arithmetic, religious practices, and Jewish history.

Not all twelve returned to Ethiopia. A few, Zimna included, had remained in Israel. Slowly, as we grew to know each other better, Zimna revealed himself. But at that first meeting, all I knew about him was that in 1979 he had joined the staff of the Jewish Agency in charge of the Ethiopian Jews, and that he had made a name for himself in Sudan, working with Mossad to secretly smuggle Jews out of the refugee camps. I had no clue of the difficulties he had faced.

We walked together out onto the embassy grounds. He

pointed a finger at the hilltop, where more than a hundred people of all ages were waiting. They looked tired. Their clothes were torn. They were sickly and thin.

"These are new arrivals from Gondar," Zimna said. "People are still coming in from distant villages. We are checking their eligibility."

"What do you mean?" I was surprised that their Jewishness needed verification.

"We work from a 1976 census of Ethiopian Jews done by the ORT"—the Organization for Vocational Training and Skilled Trade. "For those who weren't registered, we consult the *kessim*, the elders, on whether or not they're Jewish."

"It sounds complicated."

"You have no idea!" Zimna lifted his hands and raised eyes heavenward, a gesture so typically Jewish and so seemingly anomalous in his dark face that I laughed in spite of myself. He winked at me, and we were friends.

"Where do these new arrivals go once they're registered?"

"There's a line for money, a line for housing and living expenses, based on family size, and a line to receive an ID sticker. After that there's the line for food allocation."

"*Oy gevalt!*"

"You said it. But what else can we do? These are simple people from the villages. They don't mind waiting. Look how patient they are."

We walked away from the hill. There were perhaps a thousand people in the embassy and surrounding grounds. Despite the crowds there was very little hubbub. Their quietness amazed me. Children didn't cry; parents talked in soft voices. There were no arguments. They waited patiently on line without pushing. How different from Israelis, who would have been impatient, bickering among themselves. These people seemed to have the forbearance of Job. I wondered how they would fare on the streets of Jerusalem and Tel Aviv.

The smell of manure mixed with the scent of wood smoke. Zimna explained that the smoke came from lunch preparation for the children who attended the school on the embassy grounds. I asked to see the school. We walked through cypress groves where the Beta Israel murmured respectful greetings to Zimna. The children who had recently come from Gondar were an unsettling sight with their dirt-caked shreds of clothing and thin faces; their eyes were filled with pus and rimmed with flies.

"These people must have had a very difficult time before they got to Addis."

Zimna nodded. "They arrived with nothing—tired, sick, hungry, with little or no money. They abandoned their homes. They had nothing to sell—some ceramic pots for water and cooking. They were able to sell their animals—most families owned a bull for plowing, cows, and sheep. But we Beta Israel were prohibited from owning land, just like Jews in Europe during the Middle Ages. What little money they got for selling their animals they spent coming here. Food in Ethiopia is rationed, distributed through *kabele* shops in each neighborhood. Jews are not eligible for rations because they are not Addis residents, so we distribute food. Each person receives a monthly ration of five kilograms of wheat, one and a half kilos of beans, and a half liter of corn oil. This is free. In addition, people are entitled to buy other products—coffee, salt, tea, sugar, and soap—at subsidized prices at special shops financed by the JDC, which we have opened at the embassy. But before assistance is given, all new arrivals must go to the clinic."

"I have never managed an embassy like this," I said.

"This is not just an embassy," he said. "This is a small city and you are mayor!"

"What! It's not enough now to be ambassador. I have to be mayor, too!"

Zimna looked out over the bustling compound. "You know, Asher, I have waited a long time for this. After thirty years of work to help the Beta Israel emigrate, I think I have finally found a partner."

I took his hand. "Zimna, it's a blessing to work with you."

PHANTOM FIGHTERS

The best form of prayer is work.

—*Israel Zangwill*

Zimna led me to a grove of eucalyptus where the school had been set up—not one school building as I had expected, but a series of large round structures with thatched roofs (called *tukuls*, the traditional building method in the Ethiopian countryside), open on their sides. The children came three times a week for four hours and received a meal and a shower (a kitchen and shower area were specially built for this purpose; the showers were, for many of these kids, their first). They were served, perhaps, their only nourishing meal of the day—a roll, potato, hardboiled egg, and an orange. Twenty-three *tukuls* accommodated four thousand youngsters of all ages in four shifts. It was the largest Jewish school in the world. There were more than fifty kids in each class. They sat at long wooden benches. They had obviously come to school eager to learn and were extremely attentive to their teachers.

The school taught Hebrew, Amharic, and arithmetic. Zimna

introduced me to Headmaster Jacob Elias Asnako. Asnako had been part of the second group of young people who came to Kfar Batia in 1956. Unlike Zimna, he had returned to Ethiopia to teach at the "combined" Ethiopian government and Jewish Agency school that had opened in Ambover, near Gondar at the end of the 1960s. In 1978, he was accused of being a Zionist spy and imprisoned for four years.

"These people were sadists," he said. "Every morning they'd bring me before the commandant. 'Admit you're a traitor,' he would say. I would deny it. Then they'd beat me with a stick."

"Why didn't you make a false confession?" I asked.

"Because then they would have killed me."

"It sounds like the gulag. Like Solzhenitsyn."

"That's exactly how it was."

"How it is," I said.

"Hush," said Asnako softly and put his forefinger to his lips.

"SHALOM," THE ETHIOPIAN teachers quietly greeted me. Their courtesy was grave; their pride quiet, based on a kind of grace. It was a constant lesson in Ethiopia—one can be poor and still possess a rich culture.

A little girl with a round face and bright eyes ran up to me. "Shalom! Shalom!" she said. Zimna introduced her as Rivka, and her mother, standing nearby with her eyes demurely down and a pleased shy smile on her face, as Yehudit.

"Shalom to you, Rivka," I said in Hebrew, and she came forward and threw her arms around my leg.

"Jerusalem! Jerusalem!" she sang, and she kept singing the word and smiling. Playmates around her took up the chant. And then the adults joined in, all looking at me now with fervor and longing in their eyes. "*Jerusalem!*" I felt myself shaken where I

35

stood. Their single-minded concentration was apparent, focused on this one aim, one target, one ambition—to go to Jerusalem. Their longing pierced me. These people had suffered and endured to keep the faith we shared.

"I, too, come out of Africa," I said to Zimna. "The son of a barber from Tripoli." He was now looking at me in a new way. "I was the one who convinced my parents to emigrate to Israel in 1944. Four and a half years later, when I was seventeen, I forged my birth date to be accepted in the draft and fight in the war of independence. I was always a Zionist."

"The army is a great melting pot, as I'm sure these little ones will find," Zimna said. Then he looked at me oddly. "But you know when I really began to think like an Israeli?"

"When you got chutzpah!"

"Not quite," he laughed. "During Operation Moses, the Israeli navy mounted rescue operations to bring Ethiopian Jews out of Sudan. In January 1982, we had trucked about 350 emigrants out of the refugee camps to the coast, a grueling trip that took almost all night. We arrived before dawn to meet a navy ship, surreptitiously moored offshore on a desolate stretch of coastline. They were waiting for us and sent small boats in, and we managed to ferry our human cargo aboard. It all went smoothly. We were as quiet as could be, working like thieves in the night. The plan was for this vessel to move north through the Red Sea into the Gulf of Aqaba and land in Eliat—a thirty-hour trip. There was a sick little girl aboard; she must have been about six. Her mother found me. I took them straight to the ship's clinic. When I returned I found the mother holding the girl on her lap crying. The father sat next to them with wet eyes. They hadn't been able to enter the infirmary because so many people needed medical help. The journey from Ethiopia to Sudan had been brutal for many of these people, and months or even years in the harsh conditions of the refugee camps hadn't helped. I felt the girl's forehead. It was blazing with fever. She was shaking uncontrollably, her eyes rolled back in her head. I took her in my arms and went into the infirmary and in one minute she was in the hands of a young Israeli doctor. When he examined her he chastised me for not bringing her earlier. After consultation with another doctor he decided she was suffering from meningitis. They administered medicine, but it had no effect. The boat was speeding northward, the sun high overhead. I remember how exhausted I was, how the feeling of jubilation at knowing my people had escaped, and were heading toward a new life, was tempered by the little girl who hovered at the edge of death and her sobbing parents. And then something happened that it was hard for me as an Ethiopian to comprehend.

" 'The girl needs to be evacuated,' the doctor said. 'Come with me. I'm going to speak to the captain.'

"We raced upstairs to the bridge. 'We need a helicopter to evacuate a six-year-old girl who is in danger,' the doctor said.

" 'Impossible,' the captain replied. 'We are between Sudan and Saudi Arabia, enemy territory. It's too dangerous!'

" 'I don't care. We need a helicopter.'

" 'Don't you realize that could provoke an international incident? I won't do it!'

" 'Then let this girl's death be on your conscience. I demand you send a cable to navy headquarters requesting a helicopter or that you give me in writing that you take full responsibility for the fate of this girl.'

"The cable was sent. I was flabbergasted. I had spent months in Sudanese refugee camps. I had grown up in Ethiopia. I knew how cheap life can be. People perishing of sickness, famine. Nobody cares. In the context of my culture, the argument between the doctor and the captain was surreal.

"What followed was even more surreal. The captain told us the request had gone up the ladder of command to the minister of defense, who consulted with Prime Minister Begin. Next I heard that Begin had given the green light for the helicopter to be dispatched. Because of the danger, he had ordered it accompanied by two Phantom fighter jets. I couldn't believe it! The danger and expense! All to save the life of one girl. What a crazy country, I thought. But in the next moment it all made sense to me and I finally knew what it was to be Israeli."

We were silent a moment. "What a story!" I finally said. "It reminds me of what the Talmud says: 'Saving a life is saving the world' and *'Kol israel arevim ze laze,'* all Jews are their brother's keepers."

We looked at each other with warmth and shook hands. Zimna had to go back to helping his people adjust to their new surroundings and prepare for their great journey to the Promised Land that I was supposed to arrange. As I went back into the embassy I sensed the atmosphere of mission that gripped the embassy. Israelis are usually busy building their egos and scrutinize each other with critical eyes. But in Addis I was surrounded by esprit de corps—a recognition that we were inside an unfolding historic event.

SEVEN

LEAKS

Birds are entangled by their feet and men by their tongues.

—*Thomas Fuller*

Soon after I arrived in Addis, I was asked to present my credentials to Mengistu. His envoy and four assistants came to my suite at 9:00 A.M. Maimon and Micha Feldman of the Jewish Agency accompanied me. I was very happy to be working with Feldman again. He had been working with Beta Israel since the late 1970s, and he was one of the few Israelis I knew who spoke fluent Amharic, enjoyed Ethiopian cuisine, and knew all about the Beta Israel *mishpachologia*, family tree.

I was astounded when Micha showed up at the hotel wearing shorts and sandals—he was really a kibbutznik to his teeth. He kvetched when I forced him into trousers, a jacket, and a tie that Adanich pulled from my closet.

Six police motorcyclists, a Cadillac, and two Mercedes were waiting for us outside the Hilton, Ethiopian and Israeli flags fluttering on their hoods. Feldman and Maimon went into the

Mercedes; I was given the Cadillac. Three of the motorcycles swung out in front and switched on loud sirens. All traffic stopped as we made our way to the palace and pedestrians stared in awe.

The pomp and circumstance of the diplomatic world often annoyed and embarrassed me. And it became absurd in a place like Addis—limos on streets fit for mules, the country crumbling, most of the population living in hovels.

Thank goodness the palace was only a five-minute drive from the hotel. We were let out at its entrance, at the head of a double line of soldiers in spotless military garb, holding their gleaming rifles at arm's length vertically out in front of them. The commander detached himself from the unit, saluted, and walked to the side and a little behind me as I toured the ranks. When I had passed, we saluted each other.

Mrs. Sheune was waiting for us on the palace steps. She led me to Mengistu.

"Welcome to Ethiopia," he said. We sat down on couches together and made chitchat. It was all fairly soporific. Soon I was out in the lovely air, about which I was very glad. The night before an incident had occurred that had jeopardized my relationship with Mengistu and put the Beta Israel at risk.

CAN ONE FEED a lion grass? No, he expects meat! So it was with Mengistu. We had been trying to keep him happy. We met with Kasa and peppered him with goodwill gestures: irrigation projects, investors from Britain interested in Ethiopian textiles, a provision for hospital treatment in Israel of injured Ethiopian generals, equipment for a water purification plant on Dahlak Island. We never said no when he demanded money or arms. It was my job when I talked to him to subtly convey that we would have liked to help, but were hampered by Washington—and that a special American envoy, at our behest, was due to arrive in Addis soon.

In the meantime, however, the military struggle against the Eritrean rebels had spread to other Ethiopian tribes, and the Butcher of Addis was growing desperate. Kasa was granting fewer and fewer Beta Israel visas. He was squeezing us.

Two DAYS BEFORE, I had been visited by the four-member Israeli parliamentary subcommittee that handled issues pertaining to Ethiopian Jews. That all the members came was an indication of the intense political interest in Israel in the Falashas. Likkud delegate Ovadia Eli had emigrated to Israel from Morocco and built his political base as mayor of the northern city of Afula before he was elected to the parliament. Jacob Tzur represented the left-of-center socialist party. Short, in his early sixties with gray hair and sharp eyes, Tzur was a dedicated idealist from the old guard. And then there was Shimeon Shitrit.

In his early forties, Shitrit was a law professor at Hebrew University. He was an ambitious Jerusalemite and sought to take a position of leadership by "confirming" the scheduled meetings and claiming to "head" the delegation, a questionable title that was ignored by Ovadia and Tzur.

The delegates landed at 11:00 A.M., and all that they wanted to do was see their long-lost brethren. They literally threw their suitcases to the Hilton's porter, and off we drove to the embassy. Their excitement peaked when they beheld the Falashas. They wanted to speak to them, but could only say "Shalom! Jerusalem!"

I could hardly believe that Ovadia, normally a tough politician, was awash in sentiment. I wondered where the political will had been in the 1960s and 1970s, when it might have been relatively easy to extract the Ethiopians but few Israeli politicians had been interested in them. Was the will lacking at that time because the Beta Israel were black? Was it because we had doubted their Judaism?

I had thought it was because Israel had enough to do—fighting five wars, gathering 120 different communities from all over the world, building a nation. But I had my doubts now, seeing the politicians leaning forward, talking in dulcet tones, laying fond fingers upon black arms and shoulders. They were wrapped in a self-induced aura of mission, magic, destiny fulfilled.

They went back to the Hilton, lavish in their praise of the Beta Israel. "A kind, gentle people," they gushed. "Lovely! Beautiful! So quiet and polite!" They dined well on the Hilton buffet and fell into the comfortable beds on upper floors of the hotel's main building, the dimly lit metropolis spread out beneath them.

The next day, I had them meet various Ethiopian politicos. All seemed to be going well until, at a meeting with Foreign Minister Tesfaye Dinka, Shitrit asked whether it would be possible to increase the number of Beta Israel emigrants. The foreign minister, wanting to appear cooperative, assured him that Beta Israel would be allowed to leave in large numbers.

"How many?" Shitrit asked.

"As many as you want," Dinka replied. As many as you want for the right price was what he meant.

I HAD NO idea that this exchange had occurred until I got a call that night. On the way back from the theater in Jerusalem, Haim

Divon had seen the early edition of the *Jerusalem Post*. When he called me at 11:45 P.M., I was asleep. It had been a full day.

"Asher," Divon said, "I am holding the early edition of the *Jerusalem Post* and the headline reads that Foreign Minister Dinka has promised the emigration of thousands of Beta Israel."

I tried to clear my head. "The government has made no such promise. Kasa and crew are going to be furious when they read the article. How did this happen?"

Divon read me the article, which quoted Shitrit, and it didn't take us long to figure out what had occurred. Shitrit, after meeting with Dinka, had called his press office and issued a statement that not only made it sound as though he was the bearer of glad tidings but implied that his astute and persuasive presence on the ground in Addis had effected this minor miracle.

"This is a disaster," I said. "I present my credentials to Mengistu tomorrow. And I don't know how I can face Kasa." I was fully awake now—and angry. "Kasa harps on the fact that all we're interested in is the Falashas—that we care nothing for Ethiopia. That is why I arranged meetings with Shitrit and crew with various branches of the government. That is why we have just established friendship associations in both parliaments—all in vain!"

"We briefed them at the ministry before their departure," Divon said.

"Call the paper and tell them to suppress the report. It will hurt our efforts to help Beta Israel emigrants. It places us in conflict with the Ethiopian government!"

Divon sighed. "Asher, where do you think you are? Do you want a bigger disaster? On top of it all do you want the headlines to read: 'Government Tries to Interfere with Freedom of the

Press'? Talk to Shitrit and see what he has to say. I'm afraid damage control is up to you."

I dressed and called Shitrit. He didn't answer his phone. The guards outside my room were sleeping, slumped in their chairs, rifles leaning up against the wall. They didn't wake as I slipped out, and I remembered David's *"bubot"* comment. I walked through the hotel's empty corridors. Everywhere was quiet.

Shitrit was at the reception desk on the phone. I hoped he was not giving more interviews! I rushed over to him: "Jerusalem just called and woke me with an account of your press release." And I told him the headline.

"I didn't tell my assistant to publish anything," he said.

"Spokesmen publicize their boss's activities!" I was having a hard time remaining calm and polite. "That's their job. This puts us in a terrible situation with the Ethiopian government. We need their goodwill for Falasha emigration."

I saw him deflate as he realized his mistake. He suddenly seemed very tired and rubbed his eyes with the back of his hand and sighed. "I didn't mean it to come out that way. *Mode veozev, yeruham"*—forgive one who admits a mistake.

With that, my anger disappeared. "We'll do what we can," I told him, and we said good night.

POLITICIANS EVERYWHERE ARE the same. They play to the gallery. They are public personalities who compete to be reelected. Diplomats, on the other hand, are mostly civil servants. They work behind closed doors. The contents of their negotiations are often secret. Diplomacy is the glue that holds fragile alliances together. It is discreet, civilized, and it is not self-serving.

The guards were still asleep when I got back to my suite. They stirred briefly as I let myself in. Why wake them? I wondered as I passed how they perceived this exodus of Jews, the strangers in their midst, back to the Zion that in their culture's eyes had lost its sanctity, and God's favor, millennia ago. Two small people on the periphery of the action. My Rosencrantz and Guildenstern, heads lolling, chins settling back upon their chests.

EIGHT

A GLASS OF WATER

I am black but comely, O ye daughters of
Jerusalem, as the tents of Kedar, as the curtain of
Solomon. . . .

—The Song of Songs

The next morning, I found the expected message: "Kasa
called." After breakfast, I took a deep breath and went to
see him in his office at the ministry.

"We have lodged an official protest," said Kasa, right off.
"Dinka is fuming."

"Kasa, I'll try to find out about this and let you know."

Then, before my eyes, Kasa transformed. His anger was
replaced by a wry look and a humorous grin. With a twinkle in his
eye, he said, "An auspicious beginning! Did Moses deal with press
leaks?" Suddenly he was my friend, a co-conspirator, a brother in
arms, subtly reminding me that there was a certain distance we
could walk together before we clashed. His ability to toy with my
emotions was superb.

• • •

AFTER KASA, I went to see Zimna at the "men's house," where seven *shlichim* lived. The house was in a nice (for Addis) neighborhood in Bole, full of tall flowering hedges and palm trees. It was comfortable, built of stone, with a large living room and kitchen. In the living room was a long table that could seat twenty-five. The maid-cook was serving breakfast to both men and women who came from the adjacent "women's house." The *shlichim* took their meals at the men's house because it was bigger.

"There are more men *shlichim* than women here," Zimna explained. "It's a tough place for women. They can't go out at night alone. They can't sit by themselves in a coffee shop."

"He's exaggerating, of course," said a tall slim woman with black hair that fell in ringlets to her shoulders. When she smiled, she revealed rows of gleaming white teeth. Zimna introduced me. "This is Ester, a colleague from the Jewish Agency, or, should I say, our Queen of Sheba!"

I learned that Ester had immigrated to Israel from Ethiopia several years earlier. She had done well for herself, becoming the head accountant of an ambulance service. Unlike her compatriots, she talked straight and to the point, just like an Israeli woman. Her black eyes were bright. She moved quickly, and her long skirt, wide at the bottom, twisted when she moved.

We breakfasted on fried eggs, cheese, jam, and homemade bread. Ester poured coffee so strong that I needed a big dose of milk to tame it down.

"I have heard that the Beta Israel have their own version of the Solomon and Sheba story," I said.

"We certainly do," Ester replied.

Zimna jumped in. "Let me tell it to you the way I heard it when I was a child." Ester scoffed, but Zimna continued. "Sheba, the legend goes, was an Ethiopian queen. We Ethiopians have a slightly different version of the Solomon and Sheba story than appears in the Bible."

I knew the passage Zimna was referring to—Kings 10:1–12.

The Queen of Sheba arrived in Jerusalem with a very great caravan with camels carrying spices, large quantities of gold, and precious stones. She came to Solomon and talked with him about all that she had on her mind.

Solomon answered all her questions; nothing was too hard for the king to explain to her.

When the Queen of Sheba saw the wisdom of Solomon and the palace he had built, the food on his table, the seating of his officials, the attending servants in their robes, his cup-bearers, and the burnt offerings he made at the temple of the Lord, she was overwhelmed.

The Biblical story ends when both Solomon and Sheba exchange presents. But, Zimna explained, Ethiopians say that Sheba slept with Solomon, returned to Ethiopia, and gave birth to Menelik, Solomon's son.

"Tell me about this seduction!" I said.

"Solomon," said Zimna, "as you know, was a great womanizer. Tell me, how could he resist an Ethiopian queen? Can you imagine her? Draped in leopard skins, gold, and ivory. Black and long-limbed like our lovely Ester!"

Ester laughed and gave him a playful punch on the shoulder.

"Solomon, of course, asked her to stay in his palace," Zimna continued.

" 'I will stay,' she said. 'But you cannot touch me against my will.' (She had, doubtless, heard of his reputation).

" 'I agree,' said Solomon. 'But don't take anything that's mine, or you'll have to do something for me in return.'

"The wise king fed her a dinner full of hot, salty food and then put a pitcher of water and a glass on a table near her bed. Sheba awoke thirsty in the middle of the night and had herself a drink. Solomon appeared, pointing out that she had drunk his water.

" 'It's only water,' said the queen.

" 'And what is water? The most important thing in world,' he replied.

" 'Let me finish my drink and I'll do everything you desire,' she said and came into his bed and spent the night with him.

"She is reported to have said to Solomon, 'From this moment I will not worship the sun but the creator of the sun, the God of Israel.' "

"When did she say that?" I asked. "Before or after?"

"That's not the point," said Zimna. "The point is that she adopted Judaism, and began the ancient bond that exists between Israel and Ethiopia. Sheba, as you may have guessed, returned to Ethiopia pregnant and gave birth to Menelik. When he was a boy, she sent him to Jerusalem to learn from his father. He lived in Solomon's palace until he became a man. Solomon then sent him back to Ethiopia accompanied by seventy warriors from all tribes of Israel. According to the legend, before he left, he stole the Ark of the Covenant from the Holy of Holies on Mount Zion. Then, on the way back to Ethiopia, there was a river to cross on Friday evening. Those who crossed became Ethiopian Christians. Those who refused to cross, because of Shabbat, became the Beta Israel."

"So you proved you were good Jews by not crossing the river."

"Exactly," said Zimna.

"And still we wouldn't cross!" said Ester.

"What happened to the Ark?" I asked.

Zimna pondered. "The Christians say that it's kept in Axum at the Church of Zion."

"Do you think it's there?"

"Of course not!"

"Why did Solomon send Menelik away?"

" 'Two kings cannot rule in one place,' he told Menelik."

"So it was a friendly parting of the ways?"

Zimna nodded.

"Then why did Menelik steal the Ark?"

"He wanted to build a new Jerusalem," said Zimna, "in Ethiopia."

"Madam," I said to Ester, "what do you think of the Solomon and Sheba story?"

"Utterly ridiculous," she said. "But one thing in it is true."

"And what's that?"

"The attraction of Israeli men to Ethiopian women. That has certainly been my experience!"

And with that she rose from the table.

"More coffee, gentlemen?" She turned on her heel, and winked at me over her shoulder, her skirt snapping around her hips.

NINE

A DROP OF BLOOD

They suffer from calumny of being called *budas*,
sorcerers who eat the flesh of living people and at
night turn into hyenas to kill their neighbor's
cattle.

—*Jacques Faitlovitch to King Menelik II*

Ester exuded a saucy confidence, but, as I learned over innumerable cups of coffee, she had met a number of personal tragedies in Israel. Her only daughter had died in an elevator accident, and her husband beat her. He had come with her through Sudan in Operation Moses and couldn't cope with the new reality of life in Israel. He had become incensed and then depressed after the Israeli rabbinate had questioned the Falashas' Judaism.

"Why was that?" I asked.

Zimna and Ester sighed in unison.

"It's complicated," said Zimna. And he told me, in rough outline, the following story.

THE JEWISH WORLD had first learned about the Falashas from a report by the London Missionaries for the Conversion of Jews in the 1860s, which had found Jews in Ethiopia and tried, unsuccessfully, to convert them.

The Alliance Israelite Universelle in Paris heard about the London Missionaries' report, which the expedition had produced upon their return to England, and raised ten thousand francs from French and English Jews to send Professor Joseph Halevy to Ethiopia to investigate.

Halevy, a French Jewish scholar who knew Amharit, made the arduous journey into the Simians. He came to the isolated villages with Stars of David painted on the doors and ceilings of synagogues that were little more than thatched huts. He saw the Orit, the five books of Moses, which were holy to the Beta Israel. He saw how strictly observant they were of the rites and rituals of Judaism, and he learned how they had kept their faith through the centuries, in the face of persecution, ostracism, and isolation. How could anyone, especially a Jew, remain unmoved by this?

The Beta Israel, for their part, couldn't believe at first that Halevy was a Jew. Their isolation was so profound that, at that point, they thought they were the last Jews on earth. When Halevy learned this, he was thunderstruck. To maintain and practice their faith, believing they were the last remnant! Judaism has many extraordinary instances of this kind of devotion, of the survival of a people in the face of incredible odds, but nowhere more so than in the mountains of Ethiopia.

And the Beta Israel? What were their feelings when they learned they weren't alone?

"We wanted to reunite with our people," Zimna said.

"How do you know?" I asked.

"I know."

That was the beginning. Halevy's disciple, Jacques Faitlovitch, opened a Jewish school in Addis in 1924. The Jewish Agency (which started in the late nineteenth century as an arm of the international Zionist movement to help Jews) opened its first Jewish school in Asmara, Eritrea, in 1954. The school had thirty-three students, including seven *kessim*. By 1956, more Jewish schools were operating in Ethiopia. Also, in the 1950s, twenty-seven teenagers, Zimna among them, were schooled in Kfar Batia. But they came not as emigrants or recognized Jews but as students on visas. The rabbinic establishment saw them as *safek* Jews—a Talmudic term meaning "doubtful."

By the early 1970s, there was a movement of Beta Israel who wanted to emigrate to Israel, although they were still not recognized as Jews, which would have entitled them to make *aliyah*. More than one hundred Ethiopian Jews were living in Israel, and, although not known to the general public, they had become a cause célèbre for some liberal Israeli intellectuals. It was an era of severe famine in Ethiopia and a movement began, demanding that the government resolve the status of the Beta Israel as Jews and rescue our lost tribe from starvation.

In particular, Hezy Ovadia of Tzahala led this movement. Ovadia was hardly an intellectual. In fact, he was a career military man, a prototypical sergeant major with a bristling handlebar mustache who barked orders and whose word was law. He was never without his baton. God help the hapless soldier who gave him flak. His undisguised joy at making life hell for recruits had made him something of a public personality. Photos of him, looking particularly fierce, were tacked to the walls of many barracks.

Ovadia, a Yemenite Jew, had been born and raised in Ethiopia. He had made *aliyah* in the mid-1930s. He had relatives among the Falashas, who pressured him to help them emigrate to Israel. He initiated a meeting with Chief Rabbi Ovadia Yoseph, a Sephardic Jew, and presented him with the report of ha-Dani, a ninth-century traveler, and the ruling of Rabbi David Ben-Zimra (RADBAZ), the chief rabbi of the Jewish community in Egypt in the sixteenth century, both of whom recognized Beta Israel as Jews from the tribe of Dan.

In particular, the Ben-Zimra ruling was significant. He was considered the greatest authority on *halacha* (Jewish law) in the world at the time. An Abyssinian woman who claimed that she and her sons were Jewish was brought before him. She and her sons had been captured in battle, her husband murdered, and then she had been redeemed by an Egyptian Jew. Her sons now wanted to marry within Egypt's Jewish community. She testified that she belonged "to the Israelite kingdom on the mountain of Abyssinia."

Ben-Zimra accepted her story. "It is well known," he ruled, "that there are always wars among the kings of Abyssinia where there are three kingdoms—one Arab, one Aramaic [Christian], and one Israelite of the tribe of Dan."

The inside joke was that the master sergeant had nudged and bullied the chief rabbi (those who knew Hezy said this was not at all out of the question). The rabbi had finally thrown up his hands and said, Enough already!, and in 1973 issued the following ruling on the two documents Hezy presented.

These Falashas are unquestionably of the Tribe of Dan . . . and they are Jews whom we are commanded to redeem and revive. In the matter of genealogy alone is there cause for fear . . . the Falashas are Jews whom we are obliged to save from assimilation and whose return to Eretz Israel we must expedite. We must educate them in the spirit of our holy Tora and involve them in building our holy Land: "And Thy children shall return to their own border." (Jeremiah 31:17). . . . To save a single Jewish soul is to save an entire world. . . . May it be G-d's will that Isaiah's prophecy come to pass: "and the ransomed of the L-rd shall return, and come with singing unto Zion, and everlasting joy shall be upon their heads. And it shall come to pass in that day, that the L-rd will set His hand again the second time to recover the remnant of His people . . . and they shall worship the L-rd in the holy mountain at Jerusalem."

The ruling gave the government the basis to grant, in 1975, the Beta Israel the right to make *aliyah* with all the privileges that entails—full rights as citizens, help with absorption into Israeli society, support with housing and finding a job, a monthly stipend, and a guaranteed standard of living far beyond anything imaginable in Ethiopia. Hezy's relatives made *aliyah*. Hezy had gotten his way.

But other rabbis put forward reservations as to "In the matter of genealogy alone there is cause for fear." They began to make a stink, and in 1985—when Ester and her husband had recently arrived in Israel—the rabbinate declared that Beta Israel males needed to undergo *hatafat dam b'rit*, token circumcision in which the penis is nicked with a traditional knife and a drop of blood taken as an offering to God to mark his covenant with Abraham—this even though each Beta Israel man had been circumcised on the eighth day after birth, according to Jewish law. Since the rabbis had no history of the Beta Israel's roots, their ancestry was suspect.

The rabbis' degree of skepticism was, perhaps, exaggerated. Some observers suspected it was there because the Beta Israel were black. Russian Jews did not undergo the same scrutiny, even though many were "suspect Jews." As ambassador to Finland from 1988 to 1990, I know for a fact that fully 25 percent of the Russians who entered Israel under the Law of Return are not considered Jews in accordance with *halacha*.

The first Beta Israel arrivals had their *shlongs* put to the knife in assembly-line fashion. I would hear about this from a Beta Israel who was there and dropped his pants like the rest. "We didn't know what was going on," he said. "We were just so glad to be in Israel, among our people."

THE *HATAFAT DAM* procedure was done on the first Beta Israel who came from Ethiopia in the early 1980s. It was done by a local rabbi in Atlit near Haifa. When this was revealed, it was stopped. But the news traveled fast.

The Beta Israel were deeply hurt. "Our worst enemies," wrote Ben Irabhan, who had come to Israel in 1950s with Zimna, in *The Jewish Chronicle*, "never imagined such a painful way to hurt us as the wound inflicted by our own brethren."

Thousands of Ethiopian Jews converged on Jerusalem and marched on parliament, Prime Minister Yitzhak Rabin's office, and the chief rabbinate's headquarters. It was very unlike these gentle people, who had grown up in a society and culture where demonstrations were forbidden. Their protests did have some results. The Israeli public became aware of the Ethiopians' treatment at the hands of the rabbinate, which gradually acceded and eased their demands. Conversion became a simple ritual. Beta Israel went to the *mikvah* and that was that. The rabbis couldn't back down completely and still save face. But they bowed.

"MY HUSBAND COULDN'T reconcile himself to the *b'rit*," Ester said. "He went to the *mikvah*, but he came back fuming and fell into a funk. After suffering so much for being Jewish in Ethiopia, now he has to suffer, too, for being a Jew in Israel."

"But this *mikvah* wasn't the reason you had so much trouble with your husband," said Zimna. He turned to me. "Her husband couldn't reconcile himself to Ester's success. She earned more than he did in his job as a security guard. It made him bitter. He beat her and then she separated from him."

"I often hear of this," I said. "Friction between husbands and wives in Israel's Ethiopian community."

Zimna nodded. "The change in the Ethiopian woman's status in Israel is too fast, too radical. The Ethiopian man's role as the most important figure in the family and in the society is being threatened."

"Women can survive on their own," Ester said. "They make their own choices in Israel." She stood up. "Now, gentlemen, I must run to the clinic. Patients are waiting. Come and see," she said to me. "We are saving lives there." With that she gave me a kiss on both cheeks and rushed out.

NOVEMBER IS A beautiful month in Addis. The sun was shining, the sky a bright and cloudless blue. I sent Konata on ahead with the Peugeot to the embassy and rode with Zimna in the Jeep.

"It must have been painful for you when the rabbis doubted your Judaism," I said. "Did you go to the *mikvah*?"

"That was not the proudest moment of my life, but I wanted to have it behind me," he said with a bitter smile.

"Be careful of the pothole!" I yelled at him, but it was too late, and the Jeep jumped heavily up and down.

"Sorry," he said. "It was either the pothole or the goat." His smile had returned.

"Do you know what made the rabbis take that position?" I asked.

"Yes, I know. I made it my business to know. The rabbis say they lack testimony of the origin of Beta Israel. There is no written evidence by any of our ancestors or archaeological evidence. They don't know who we are and where we are from."

"What do you mean?"

"They say we are a people without a history. The stories about us are *agadot*, legends with no proof. On legends alone, they say, they can't make judgments. That is why there is 'doubt.' "

I respected Zimna's dispassionate analysis. He paused to let his words sink in.

We had come to the embassy. The guard let us through the gate and we drove up the hill to the embassy building itself, surrounded as usual by lines of Beta Israel and people running to and fro. Zimna made to get out of the Jeep, but I stopped him with a hand on his arm. I knew there were countless phone calls I needed to return, and dozens of people waiting to see me. But hearing Zimna out seemed more important.

"The second problem," he continued, "is the question of marriage with Jews. The rabbis say that since we lived a pre-Talmudic system of rules that governed marriage and divorce, there is *safek mamzer*, that is, doubts of bastardness. Do you know what *bastard* means in Judaism?"

"Not really."

"Bastardness is defined only in one case: when a child is born to a couple forbidden to marry, such as a child born from incest or where a married woman gives birth to a child not from her husband. A child born to a single maiden or to a divorced woman is not considered a bastard. Now the rabbis say that since we may not have known the rules of marriage and divorce, divorce of married women may not be legal. So a child from her second husband may be a bastard in the eyes of the rabbinical law."

This was becoming complicated. In Israel, recognition as a Jew is important because Personal Status Law, which includes marriage and divorce, is under the rabbinical courts. These courts rule under rabbinical law, not state law.

"Believe me, Asher, I went through this in my first marriage with Sarah," said Zimna, looking down at the floor. "I went to the *mikvah* to put it behind me."

"Oh, Zimna," I said. "It's a hard thing. But, you know, life is 10 percent what happens to us and 90 percent how we react to it."

He thought about that a moment. "You're right, Asher," he said. But there was still bitterness in his face—and I didn't blame him.

TEN

CARTE BLANCHE

The trouble you make for yourself is always
harder to deal with than the trouble others make
for you.

T he tripartite meeting was a great coup for Mengistu.
Washington agreed to send Herman Cohen, undersecre-
tary of state for African affairs, to Ethiopia. Frankly, I was
surprised at America's willingness to reinvolve itself in Ethiopia's
affairs. It was a humanitarian gesture and a show of support for
Israel. Then President George Bush's familiarity with the Beta
Israel and their plight (which stemmed from his involvement with
Operation Moses as head of the CIA in 1984) was also part of the
reason America was receptive to our overtures.

America had once been a friend to Ethiopia. Mengistu desperately wanted to rekindle that friendship. In the early 1950s, the
Americans had built the Kagnew Air Force Base in Asmara,
the capital of Eritrea (then part of Ethiopia), at the time one of
the most advanced military communications stations outside the
United States, staffed by four thousand American military personnel. Why? Because Ethiopia controlled two islands in the

middle of a narrow section of the Red Sea. Cannon placed on these islands controlled the shipping lanes of oil from the Arabian Peninsula through the Suez Canal. In return, America paid a yearly lease of twenty-five million dollars (a lot of money in those days) and was generous with Ethiopia, giving her military aid.

This relationship was engineered by Haile-Selassie, who had come to power in 1930. Haile-Selassie followed a Byzantine style of diplomacy. He avoided ceding influence to any one foreign country, while using international rivalries to promote his interests. He invited the United States, Britain, Sweden, Israel, India, and Yugoslavia to train his armed forces. Each had a discrete role. The two officer training schools, for example, were supervised by different nations: The prestigious Harar Academy was commanded by British and Indian staff while the Holeta Military Academy was staffed largely by Israelis. British officers trained Ethiopia's small navy, Swedes their air force, and Israelis their ground crews. Part of this was financed by the United States. This system distributed influence, but compromised the effectiveness of the armed forces.

After the revolution in 1974, Mengistu needed a large military arsenal to push back the Somali invasion in the south and the Eritrean rebels in the north. America, unhappy with his regime and human rights record, was reluctant to give him that kind of weaponry. In a Machiavellian move, Mengistu went to the USSR in 1977 and offered up his country in exchange for arms. Moscow viewed Ethiopia as a prize. Although poor, it was then (and, arguably, is) one of the most important countries in Africa and the symbol of Africa's independence and pride.

SINCE 1977, THE USSR and its Eastern European allies had given Ethiopia about five billion dollars in loans and aid, mostly for military equipment. Eastern European military advisers trained the Ethiopian army to use Soviet military hardware. Seventeen thousand Cubans came to Ethiopia as trainees and advisers.

The purchase of arms from the USSR was a simple matter. In the communist system, the government owned the means of production. There were no agents, go-betweens, or competition. All salaries and the price of products were dictated by the government. The price, therefore, for military hardware was much lower than in the West. Communist-bloc countries bartered for weapons. Ethiopia paid in kind, mainly with coffee and credit. It was up to the government representatives to collect the debts.

When I arrived in Addis, I found the ambassador from the USSR running around, threatening to send the Soviet advisers home unless Mengistu agreed to pay their salaries. He also was gathering signed statements of the debt owed to his country from Ethiopia's ministers of finance and defense.

The USSR would supply more arms to Mengistu only for cash payments in U.S. dollars—they wouldn't even accept rubles. And Mengistu was broke.

Cut off from the Soviets, threatened by rebels, Mengistu hoped to switch sides yet again and lure the United States back into his camp. But the Cold War was over. The United States had no special interest in Ethiopia, and Mengistu had nowhere to go. Israel was his last hope. We weren't likely to impress him, however, with our offer of a ten-million-dollar five-year aid package for agricultural development, irrigation projects, animal husbandry, and nurse training. He needed arms. The Falashas' plight was the only card he had left to play. This was the background of the tripartite meeting.

• • •

LUBRANI AND I knew that we would only have leverage if the United States offered Mengistu a carrot—an offer to mediate a political settlement between the government and the rebels and the promotion of Bob Houdek to ambassador. (The United States had recalled its ambassador when Mengistu had defected to the USSR in 1977. The American embassy in Addis was headed by a chargé d'affaires, a step that expressed indifference or dissatisfaction, bordering, in diplomacy, on an unfriendly act.)

Meanwhile, the Israeli government was under pressure. Before I left for Addis, hundreds of Ethiopian emigrants had staged demonstrations in Jerusalem, demanding that the government reunite them with their families.

Lubrani's attitude, which I thought might be optimistic, was that the meeting, the appointment of an Israeli ambassador, and the ten-million-dollar aid package would create goodwill, at least in the short term, and then we would cope with problems as they came.

BEFORE THE MEETING itself, we wanted to sound out Houdek and Herman Cohen so there would be no surprises. Lubrani, Divon, and I went to the American embassy. It was in a quiet northern part of the city, backed up against the mountains. Konata drove us past the zoo, where mangy lions lolled, and the dilapidated palace of Haile-Selassie, which had been turned into Addis Ababa University. A three-yard-high wall topped with loops of barbed wire surrounded the American compound. The embassy entrance was guarded by U.S. Marines and unarmed Ethiopian guards.

First Secretary Joe DeThomas, a tall, thin man who moved cautiously and rarely smiled, met us on the other side of the gate. He barely spoke as he led us to Bob Houdek's office. The embassy was a world inside a world, with a swimming pool, tennis court, and lavish gardens.

Houdek ushered us into his office with a great show of energy and enthusiasm. He was one of those men who always seemed to be moving. His few strands of wispy hair were rarely in place. He brushed them impatiently with restless fingers and pushed his spectacles up on the bridge of his nose. He introduced us to Cohen, a compact man in his late fifties with thick black-rimmed glasses.

"Since the Gulf crisis, the flow of arms from Iraq to the rebels has slowed," Cohen began without preamble. "But money continues to flow. And for the rebels, money, at this point, is more important than arms. They get arms as booty from Mengistu's deserting soldiers. Corrupt army officers even sell them cannon and tanks."

"The situation seems ominous," I said. "Foreign currency dwindles. Defense spending rises. Exports are down. Business stagnates. The birr's black market value is three times the official rate of exchange. Ethiopia has stopped paying its foreign debt for the first time in its history. There are shortages of gasoline and other goods. These are real problems for a country under siege."

"You should know," said Cohen, "that Washington is allergic to Mengistu. He has absolutely no credibility with us. Last time Kasa Kabede showed up in Washington, he told us the 'derg' recognized that they had made many mistakes. They had operated under pressure of Somali invasion, but now they were willing to change. Congress asked him about the twelve generals jailed in Addis for treason. Kasa promised they would stand trial—that there would be no summary executions. Kasa had just left Washington when their execution was broadcast on the news. Mengistu murdered his most experienced generals and replaced them with unqualified lackeys. Since the executions, the situation in the battlefield has deteriorated. You should know that there is no way in hell we will help prop up his tottering regime. We will demand that he stop disrupting the transportation of food to the starving regions of Ethiopia that are behind rebel lines, and that he respect human rights, including the right of the Falashas to emigrate to Israel."

"Of course, Ambassador," said Houdek, looking at me, "how you construe our involvement here is another matter."

Lubrani, Divon, and I exchanged glances. We would, perhaps, have liked a softer line, but under the circumstances this was the best we could hope for. Just the American presence would be enormously persuasive. And Houdek had just given us carte blanche to deploy it for our own ends.

ELEVEN

TWO LIONS

After lunch, we went to meet Kasa for the same purpose—to sound him out. We didn't want any surprises before the meeting.

Kasa headed two departments in the politburo: the "Cadre," charged with political indoctrination, and foreign affairs. His office was in the Workers party headquarters. We were greeted at headquarters by Tesfaye Afaworki, who introduced himself as deputy to Kasa, and Ato Argau, the Foreign Ministry's deputy director for Middle Eastern and Asian affairs. Both were in their late forties. Tesfaye wore a shabby blue suit and a wrinkled shirt. These clothes were not his everyday wear. The Workers party considered suits bourgeois—a capitalist uniform. Argau's suit, on the other hand, was neatly pressed, and he met us with a smile. Both men carried notebooks.

The lobby was shabby and dark. Paint peeled off the walls. The corridors were bare, the windows filthy, covered in dust. We filed into a narrow meeting room with a long wooden table flanked by heavy wooden chairs. During the meeting, Tesfaye and Argau were silent. Had Kasa included them to make it look like a team?

Kasa was expansive. He used our first names. It was "Asher this" and "Uri that." "How good to see all of you!" He beamed.

KASA AND LUBRANI faced off. They were two seasoned diplomats, both shrewd and worldly. Two lions.

"Kasa," Lubrani said in a calm, measured way, as though talking to a friend and equal, a confidential tone that nonetheless managed to convey respect. "The importance of this meeting is that it is being held in Addis with a high-ranking U.S. official. It is an opening, but one should not expect too much in a first meeting."

Kasa sat back. "Yes, Uri, we appreciate that."

"May I suggest that you talk about what's important for Ethiopian relations with America. I can assure you that there will be follow-up meetings."

Kasa turned to us with a benevolent expression. "Uri, we now have an ambassador. It's time to speed up the visa process for the Falashas. Your embassy will be the only channel through which application forms will be presented. We won't accept applications from American groups. From our side, Mirsha, the deputy interior minister, will be the only one to deal with applications."

I was watching Kasa carefully, his expression, the way he shuffled his papers. His eyes were alert. He was fully present. In control.

Lubrani and Kasa avoided eye contact, poised for the next move. Kasa opened his file and passed a form to Lubrani. "This will be the new application for emigration," he said. "It must be filled in by an Israeli social worker. Mirsha will have a social workers' committee to assist him in handling applications. I wish to stress that unification of families is an Israeli-Ethiopian bilateral issue, there is no linkage between family unification and other bilateral issues, and there are no quota numbers. Whoever fills in the form will be allowed to leave."

Lubrani and I exchanged looks as if to say, Where's the trick? It sounded too good to be true. Kasa must have been hiding something, but what? The Jewish Agency people would be elated with the new arrangements. They wouldn't have to go, Via Dolorosa, through the old procedure that required the Falasha to produce a number of documents, most of which he didn't have.

The first document was a birth certificate. Most Beta Israel didn't have one, since in country villages birth certificates are usually issued by the church. The second was a certificate from the income tax authority, stating that the applicant didn't owe tax. Poor villagers had never heard of taxes. The third was a certificate verifying that the applicant had paid all rent, electricity, and water bills. This was ridiculous in villages without electricity or municipal water. Fourth, the applicant had to produce a certificate from the bank that he owed no money and there were no claims against him. Most Beta Israel had never been inside a bank. Many didn't even know what a bank was! Fifth, the Beta Israel needed a certificate from the *kabele* (neighborhood committee) that he hadn't conspired against the regime and that there were no civil or criminal cases pending against him. Lastly, he had to present a letter of invitation from his relatives abroad, and a visa to the country where he was going.

These requirements imposed a tremendous burden on our *shlichim*. Each application involved endless wrangling and negotiation. This was the way that the government had effectively stalled the Beta Israel's release, and I was looking for the trick behind Kasa's new offer. I suspected something, but at that point

Kasa had outfoxed me. Only later, after its implementation, did I discover that, with this new arrangement, Kasa had tightened his grip, concentrating the visa application process in his own hands through the "social work committee." That "committee" would turn out to bedevil us, and it had one member—Kasa.

TWELVE

TRIPARTITE

The tripartite meeting was held the following afternoon at three in the same bare meeting room where we had met Kasa the day before. The Americans present were Cohen, Houdek, and DeThomas; the Israelis, Lubrani, Divon, and me; for Ethiopia, Kasa, Mirsha, deputy minister of interior, and Kasheha, who was introduced as chief of protocol.

Kasa turned on the charm for Cohen, talking to him in fluent English. "We are very happy to have you here, Mr. Cohen," he said, smiling his urbane smile. "I trust you had an easy flight, and I know you have an excellent chargé"—looking at Houdek. "Still if there's anything I can do to make your stay more interesting, please don't hesitate to ask." His words carried an aura of receptivity, effortless affection, and welcome.

"The president is elated," he continued, calling us to order. "This meeting is an important event. The Falashas' family unification has already been settled in a previous meeting." No one was surprised. After our meeting with Kasa we had briefed the Americans on this new arrangement. They took it at face value. Houdek had said our suspicions were probably unfounded, that we were reading too much into it. But we were familiar with the Byzantine diplomacy in which Ethiopians excel.

"We welcome the new family unification proposal," Lubrani said. "There may be some difficulties ahead of us but with joint efforts we shall overcome!"

Cohen gave a wintry smile: "The United States approves Israel's involvement in Africa. She can contribute significant aid in agricultural development and the promotion of democratic ideas. And even Andrew Young, who is not known to be pro-Israel, encouraged African heads of state to renew diplomatic relations with Israel. There is still much goodwill for Israel in Ethiopia, despite severed diplomatic relations." Cohen paused, studied the ceiling a moment through his black-rimmed spectacles, and took a breath. "Our position is that Ethiopia's conflict cannot be resolved by force. Neither side is strong enough to impose its views. Only political negotiations between the government and the rebels will end the conflict. We are willing to help with these negotiations, but Ethiopia needs to move toward a free economy and to improve human rights. Finally, the United States is committed to the right of the Falashas who are still here to be united with their families in Israel."

Kasa nodded through this speech, his black eyes glittering. When Cohen had sat back, Kasa moved in to fill the silence, reiterating much of what Lubrani and I had already heard in our meeting with Mengistu.

"Severing relations with Israel was imposed upon us by the Organization of African Unity. Africa's Arab states called on all members of the OAU to implement its resolution to cut relations with any state that occupies African territory. The 1973 Yom

Kippur War brought the Sinai Peninsula—part of Egypt—under Israeli control. Ethiopia, as host of the OAU, had to comply." Kasa made it sound like the most reasonable thing in the world. "Our alliance with the USSR was imposed on us by Somali aggression," he continued. "The Ethiopian revolution was fed by the campus rebellion in the West. Young people all over the world were influenced by the rebellious attitude of young people in Europe and America, who were demanding a change to a new order!" At this point, Kasa realized his weak argument, so he quickly moved the agenda. "We have reached an agreement on Falasha unification," he said, turning toward our side of the table and opening his hands in a magnanimous gesture. He studied Cohen's face. "Now we have an ambassador to deal with unification. Whoever fills in the form can emigrate. There is no quota. So I would very much hope that we will not hear anymore that the Falashas are being held hostage and that we are trading 'Jews for Arms.' I hope this meeting will justify normalizing relations with the United States. We will deliver the goods on political negotiations with the rebels, a freer economy, and steps to remedy any human rights abuses. I hope that the Americans will help to strengthen Ethiopian security, if not directly, then by removing its veto from supply from others. As you know, arms flow to the rebel forces from Arab countries."

That was a bomb we didn't expect. Tactically, Kasa may have made a mistake: He obligated Cohen to reiterate U.S. policy. "America doesn't believe in a military solution to Ethiopia's problem and objects to the supply of arms to either side," Cohen said. "America will use its influence to bring the parties together for negotiations."

I had a sinking feeling. I knew Kasa must have been desperate to ask for arms in this first goodwill meeting. But aside from this remark, the meeting went smoothly. It was over after just two hours. Nothing new was said. Another meeting was set for three months. That would give us time to verify the implementation of commitments on all sides.

The next day, before Lubrani was due to leave, we met Mengistu at the palace. We found him in excellent spirits. He professed to be grateful that the United States was ready to mediate with the rebels. And, he said, he had ordered the process of Falasha unification to proceed apace.

"If there are problems, call me!" he said, looking at me.

But no sooner had he said this than he threw a wrench in the works, noting that Falasha emigration was a "bilateral issue" and that "all economic and agricultural aid is irrelevant when a nation is threatened. The rebels will negotiate only when we are strong. We need assistance here and now to stop the rebel advance."

The bottom line was that Cohen's visit seemed to have whetted his appetite for arms. And despite Kasa's rhetoric to the contrary, we knew that the Falashas would, indeed, be held hostage as long as Mengistu believed that he could get what he wanted. The mood was subdued as I took Lubrani and Divon to the airport. We all knew what my mission was, and we knew it wasn't going to be easy.

THIRTEEN

PRANZO

In Ethiopia, there were no independent newspapers, radio, or television. News was controlled by the government. A diplomat relies on nonclassified publications, statements of political leaders, debates in parliament, research institutions, and the media for information. Much of our time is spent listening, reading, and accumulating information.

But in Addis, there was none of that. There were only four to six pages in the only English daily, the *Ethiopian Herald*, which carried puff pieces about the "people's proletariat party" and the "achievements" of the "fighters for a progressive Ethiopia." Television programming focused on Mengistu's activities and the army's victories on the battlefield. Other media gave trivial and distorted information, modeling themselves on the Albanian–North Korean style of reportage. Even in the USSR, one could learn much from diligently reading *Pravda* about internal struggles within the communist party or problems affecting the country. But in Ethiopia there was nothing.

So how was I to gather information in such a place?

Newly arrived ambassadors usually visit other ambassadors to establish professional contacts and get tips on the country. Sergio Angeletti, the Italian ambassador, was my first choice as a contact because of Italy's special relationship with Ethiopia. Italy had conquered Eritrea in 1889, been defeated by Menelik II in the battle of Adwa in 1896, conquered all of Ethiopia in 1936, and occupied the country through 1941. Libya had also been under Italian occupation from 1911 through 1944, and I had learned Italian as a child.

Meets between ambassadors are usually arranged through their secretaries, but I bypassed protocol. The day after the tripartite meeting, when I realized that clear intelligence on what was happening politically in the country would be crucial in my dealings with Mengistu, I asked my secretary to connect me directly to Angeletti.

"Thanks for answering the phone directly," I told him in Italian. "I'm a native of Tripoli, which is why I know Italian. I need your advice!"

"It would be wonderful to meet you," Angeletti said. "May I please consult my secretary so I can invite you here for lunch!"

We agreed on a time two days hence.

THE ITALIAN EMBASSY, set on a hilltop, was a ten-acre compound. Inside were a number of small one- and two-story houses, and the ambassador's residence surrounded by pools, grass, and trees.

I was greeted by a polished young man in his thirties, wearing a blue suit and white shirt. He had long, groomed black hair. I caught a glimpse of a blond secretary in a chic one-piece dress. Angeletti was a distinguished-looking man with glasses, thin and tall, in a gray suit and blue tie. Even here in Ethiopia the Italians were elegantly dressed and maintained their keen sense of fashion and design.

Angeletti took my hand and led me into his office—a far cry from mine. It was a very large room, immaculately kept, with Persian carpets on the floor.

"I have a surprise for you, Mr. Ambassador," said Angeletti. "We are lunching with my wife, Irene, who has said she knows how to prepare *hraimey*."

I politely feigned astonishment. "Where did she learn that Tripolitanian dish?"

We chatted in Italian and then moved to English, where I feel more secure. Angeletti led me to a veranda where a table was set for three. A round bosomy woman with cheeks like apples came toward me, bubbling greetings. Warmth flowed from her; her hands were rarely still. I had to laugh at this couple: he, willowy and elegant; she, a little dumpling.

Italians love long full lunches. They call them *pranzo*, a hearty meal. We started with sardines, mushroom soup, and then the *hraimey*, personally supervised by Irene—a Prince Nile fish cooked in a viscous sauce of tomatos and peppers. Chianti washed it all down.

Irene controlled the talk. She wanted to know when my wife was coming to Addis. "Tell her to be prepared! There is no supermarket here. Not even a grocery for foreigners. We fly in food from Italy with the Italian airlines. Tell her to see as many concerts as possible, because here there are none—no theater, no opera. Oh, to be Italian and not have opera!" She clutched her hands to her bosom. "This is a punishment."

After the meal, she left us.

"This is my first service in a communist country," I told Angeletti. "I was called up quickly and have come unprepared. I already feel disconnected. I have only the radio news stations from Israel, BBC, and Voice of America. None of them is preoccupied with Ethiopia, to say the least."

Angeletti poured cognac into two snifters. "The most difficult task here is to update oneself on what is going on," he said. "The media here is government controlled—like Stalin's USSR."

"So how do you get information?"

"Other ambassadors. The other day the East German first secretary personally followed a training camp for new recruits. Young people, eighteen to twenty-five, were forced into ten days of military training, then sent to the front. These recruits don't want to fight. They desert at the first opportunity. That is why Mengistu is losing so many battles. Eastern European embassies often have good information because they trained the army and supplied its weapons."

"Can you give me some background, Angeletti? Why was there a revolution in the first place? How did Mengistu wind up in this mess?"

"There is no doubt that Ethiopia was in desperate need of reform. The emperor knew this but he was at the end of his life, and incapable of making real changes. And the appointment of Lieutenant General Aman Michael Andum as prime minister was forced on him. Andum was a veteran officer, charismatic, of Eritrean origin. He had commanded the six thousand Ethiopian soldiers who took part in the Korean War. The Ethiopians fought bravely—121 died, 500 were wounded. Haile-Selassie contributed $250,000 to the war effort.

"Andum planned to set in motion changes in landownership (the emperor owned half the land in Ethiopia, the church the other half), in education, and in the way the country was governed. In February 1974, the 'derg' or military commanders took over the administration of the country from Haile-Selassie and began to implement reforms. It was a bloodless revolution."

"What kind of changes did the derg want?"

"Andum and many of his colleagues were democrats. They wanted to decentralize the government. Andum pushed to give Eritrea some autonomy. And he was going to recognize and give a measure of autonomy to all the peoples who make up Ethiopia."

"I've heard there are seventy ethnic groups."

"More!" said Angeletti. "Ethiopia is really an empire, not a country. Andum's plan would have given us stability. And now? What do we have? Bloodshed and strife."

Sadness marked Angeletti's aristocratic face. He poured more cognac and peered at the label. "This is a really good one," he said.

"What happened to Andum?" I asked.

"Mengistu hijacked the revolution. He represented military men of low rank. He promised them power. On November 23, 1974, he appeared before the derg. In an inflammatory speech, pistol in hand, with threats of violence, he bulldozed through a resolution to get rid of Andum because he was 'giving in to Eritrea.' That same night Mengistu and his men killed Andum and fifty-eight of the revolution's top leaders. By September 12, Mengistu had deposed Haile-Selassie and buried him under his desk in his office. The bloodless revolution turned bloody. The derg became brutal and despotic. Mengistu purged Ethiopia's political leaders and then went after the intelligentsia. He was left with low-ranking officers and NCOs. Those who objected to his policies were shot. Andum's dream of democratization and decentralization was dead. Ethiopia had one-man rule and a continuous war with Eritrea."

"So what's your diagnosis?"

"The revolution is coming to a close. Not if but when is the question. I only hope that the new regime will better the life of the people."

"How should we deal with the Falasha issue? Any suggestions?"

Angeletti pondered. "The more desperation you project, the higher the price they will demand. It is better to play it cool and involve others. Your government should ask the European Union's help to pressure the Ethiopian government. After all, this is a humanitarian issue *par excellence*."

Irene came in and asked if Angeletti was treating me right.

"Oh, my goodness," I said, looking at my watch. I hadn't realized that three hours had passed. I thanked them, and they accompanied me to my car. At the exit, the blond secretary showed up. Konata's mouth dropped open when he saw her. He couldn't stop staring.

"It was a pleasure," said Angeletti with his rather grave formality.

"Come back often," said the bubbly Irene.

"*Ciao!*" said the blonde.

As we drove away, I noticed Konata had trouble keeping his eyes on the road.

FOURTEEN

RED LIGHT

It was Tadese, my teacher of Amharic, who really helped me begin to cultivate my own sources of information. I always learned the language of the people where I served—to increase my understanding of what was going on around me and to open people's hearts.

Tadese had taught former ambassador Yoffe's wife. He was an English major at the university and came to lessons in jeans and sandals. He wore a gold necklace with a cross.

"How do people know what's going on at the front?" I asked.

"Not through the government."

"I know. But how?"

"The Mercato for one. It is like the old tom-tom drum with which we Africans sent message from the hilltops. People talk about what they've seen in their travels."

"Let's have our next lesson in the Mercato!"

Tadese thought a moment. "Even better than the Mercato are

the bars of Addis where the officers drink. At night, Addis becomes a red-light district. Soldiers and rebels go with the same women."

"Can you talk to them at the bars?"

"Of course."

"So let's have our next lesson there!"

Tadese gave me a long look. "It is sometimes dangerous. But I know the places well."

"It's a deal! But it's our secret. You can't tell anyone what we're doing."

His black eyes gleamed. "Yes, I promise."

It was a good arrangement. Tadese wanted someone to pay his bar bills. I wanted information and to learn what made Addis tick.

TADESE AND I set a night. Of course, I didn't tell David what I was up to. I sent Konata home early. My car was too conspicuous for a clandestine jaunt, so I asked Zimna for his Jeep. He looked at me with suspicion. I tried to throw him off the scent.

"I'm going on rough roads to visit friends. I don't want to ruin the Peugeot."

Zimna cocked his head. "Of course, Asher. I will teach your driver how to handle the Jeep."

"That won't be necessary," I said in an offhand way. "Just leave the Jeep here at the embassy with the keys. I'll handle everything."

I waited to be the last to leave the embassy. It was after seven and dark. I drove to meet Tadese, who was loitering in the shadows of the shrubbery near the Hilton's entrance. But right next to him was none other than Avi, one of the *shlichim*.

"I've been calling you in your suite, but there was no answer," he said. "So here I am!"

"Of course, Avi. Come to my suite. Here is the key. I'll join you after I park."

He looked perplexed. "But why are you driving the Jeep? What happened to your car? Did you have an accident?"

I will tell you a diplomat's secret. In a situation where you have to tell a lie or ignore the question, just ignore it. Often you won't be pressed. Offer some broad reassurance, as I did now to Avi.

"Don't worry about it. Everything is fine. Just wait for me and I'll join you soon."

Avi, as I hoped, didn't persist, and Tadese, gracefully, did not intrude. He indicated with a movement of his hand that he would stay put and wait for me.

WHEN I ENTERED my suite, Adanich was serving Avi coffee. To deflect what might be Avi's persistent curiosity about the Jeep, I initiated my own line of questioning. "Avi, how are you? I know the heavy burden on your shoulders."

He sighed. "I'm getting used to it."

"What's on your mind?" I wanted to push the point so as to end the meeting soon.

He stared into the steaming cup, not meeting my eyes. "Asher, I want to bring my wife and children here. This separation is difficult for the family. I know the situation is unstable. But my wife is a professional teacher and could help at the embassy school."

The Foreign Ministry encourages bringing whole families on foreign postings. But in unstable Ethiopia, it would be a big headache for the security people in Addis to take care of them; nevertheless, the ministry left the decision up to each of us.

"I can't advise you," I told Avi. "Advice means responsibility. If

I told you to bring your family, and, God forbid, something went wrong, I would feel responsible. It's safer in Israel. But I am bringing Hilda, my wife, next week."

Avi left happy. I sent Adanich home and sneaked past David, who was having dinner in his room. I had to ask myself if the subterfuge was worth it, and I verged on scrapping the whole idea. But my curiosity had been piqued, and the urge to experience the underbelly of Addis was overwhelming.

I WAS AT the wheel. We drove down the long hill of Menelik II Avenue, passing Lenin Square. This was my first time driving in Ethiopia, and I realized how adept Konata had been at missing potholes. I swerved to avoid a boulder in the middle of the road. How had it gotten there? It looked as though it had dropped from the sky.

Addis improved at night. Dim light hid the dirt and hovels, the shabby buildings, and the trash. Almost every block had a bar.

"This is a lower-income area," said Tadese. "Officers don't come here. The city has many different districts, all with their own character and flair."

We bumped along unpaved streets. Women stood outside their homes. In absence of streetlights, you had to come close to see them. They wore everyday clothes, normally a one-piece dress that covered them from neck to knee and short-sleeved shirts. Their appearance didn't reveal the extra "night work" they did to survive. I pitied them. Even if they had a client they made so little. Mengistu's civil war had made the poor population poorer.

We came to Teodros Boulevard, one of Addis's main roads, named after Emperor Teodros, who ruled Ethiopia from 1855 to

1868 and ushered the country into the modern era. Mengistu idolized this particular emperor.

Teodros, like Mengistu, had been born a commoner. He was educated in a monastery and then left, to lead a bandit group. The bandit group grew to become an army, and, one by one, Teodros conquered Ethiopia's warlords and united the country under a central government. He changed his name to Teodros because, in accordance with Ethiopian legend, an emperor by that name would expand Ethiopia's borders, bring prosperity to the nation, and deliver Jerusalem from Islamic rule. He established a central administration and built the foundation of a unified army, which, in the past, had depended on the soldiers of regional governors. He introduced taxation to create income for the central government. He imposed on the British missionaries to produce arms for his soldiers and built roads on which his army could move. These changes were not welcomed by all. Every change brought with it new enemies. In particular, Teodros took on the church by confiscating much of its land.

In foreign affairs, Teodros was on guard against Egypt and Sudan, which were part of the Muslim Ottoman Empire. He asked for help from Britain's Queen Victoria, but she ignored him. Teodros interpreted her lack of an answer as Britain conspiring with Ethiopia's Muslim enemies: Egypt, Turkey, and Sudan. Under this illusion, he incarcerated Cameron, the British consul, and all other British citizens, taking them hostage. Victoria responded by dispatching Lord Napier of Magdala with thirty thousand men to Ethiopia. Teodros had no chance against this modern army. In April 1868, he committed suicide.

WHEN TEODROS IS credited with leading Ethiopia into the modern era, what does that mean? In Europe it is relatively easy to grasp when one era ends and the next begins. We see great social changes during the Renaissance, the French Revolution, the Industrial Revolution, and the First World War. All are landmarks for basic social, economic, and industrial changes. But in most of Africa, and for most of African history, there is only one change of this magnitude: the colonization of the continent by European powers during the mid–nineteenth century. The European states destroyed Africa's old social, cultural, and economic order, introducing Western systems that clashed with Africa's traditions.

But the case of Ethiopia is unique and did not follow the European or African precedents. Ethiopia was the only African country to successfully resist colonization by a European power. It fought off the Italians in the battle of Adwa in 1896. The struggle of Ethiopia with colonialism renewed and rejuvenated its tradition, social structure, and religion.

MY MIND WAS so far away that I didn't hear Tadese asking me to turn right. We parked in front of a three-story house with lit windows. Soft music came from within. We mounted five steps, pushed aside a bead curtain, and entered a large room with orderly tables and freshly painted walls. The hostesses were young and well dressed.

The bar was half full. A strikingly pretty young woman in a brown dress and high heels demurely dropped her dark eyes and smilingly took me by the hand, leading me to a table in the center of the room.

Tadese was quivering with excitement. "This is one of the best bars," he said triumphantly. "It is frequented by army officers and people with money. Soldiers and NCOs don't dare come here, not only because of the social divide, but because they can't afford it!"

I wondered how much this expedition was going to cost me.

"How do you think I should introduce myself?" I asked Tadese. "An ambassador in jeans?"

There was a subdued watchfulness in the room. Money, drinks, and women were good ingredients to induce people to open up. But they would not be enough. Right then I decided to take the risky step of identifying myself. I told Tadese as much and he looked at me in a strange way. "Are you sure you want that now at the first meeting?"

"What's wrong with an ambassador looking to unwind and have a good time?" But then I thought: What happens if I meet somebody who knows me? In Israel it would be headline news the next morning.

Tadese read my mind. "Don't worry. You won't be caught in a compromising position. In Addis, sex is a private affair. It is never insinuated in public. You never see couples kissing or even holding hands. Sex is not advertised, discussed, or exhibited. We have no striptease shows. People wear decent clothes, even in a place like this."

What he said was somewhat reassuring, although I knew that just my presence here would be enough to start the tabloids singing.

Two women immediately sat down at our table and began caressing us.

"These women try to get you to pay for a drink," said Tadese in the tones of a man of the world. "They are served soda and the owner bills for alcohol. Half of that goes to the hostess. Those are the rules of the game."

"What's up there?" I asked.

"Almost every bar has private rooms," he explained. "Many of the waitresses and hostesses will oblige when invited by a customer, normally for a period of one hour. For the room you pay an extra ten birr and for the girl twenty birr. A room for the night is forty birr, for those who can't reach home because of the midnight curfew." (The curfew had been changed from nine to midnight.)

I looked around. "I don't want to be seated in such a conspicuous place," I said to Tadese.

A hostess moved us to an interior room, close to a table with a middle-aged officer and two girls. My eyes and the officer's met.

"Can I say who you are?" whispered Tadese. "This officer might be a good contact."

I nodded. He whispered in the officer's ear. The officer got up and approached me. "It is an honor to introduce myself: Colonel Asepha, armored division. You must be my guest."

Soon five beautiful, young, and seemingly bashful women were with us. But their eyes were inviting and their hands, under the table, went everywhere. A waitress took our drink order.

"Will it be *tage*, *talla*, or *kalikala*?" Asepha asked me. "Unless, of course, you want Western drinks."

"Wait a minute! I don't know about these choices."

"You are new to Addis. Marvelous! Let me tell you about our wonderful beverages. *Tage* is an alcohol made from honey, common in bars. *Talla* is kind of a beer made from barley. It is like European beer. But *kalikala* is an Ethiopian specialty made from *teff*, the staple Ethiopian grain. So what will it be?"

"I'll take the Ethiopian drink—*kalikala*!"

"*Kalikala*," said Tadese.

"We'll all have *kalikala*. Eight *kalikala* with the five girls."

I whispered to Tadese, asking him how much the drinks would cost. I wanted to make sure to pay the bill. Tadese told me that in most bars you paid one birr for two bottles, but here it was two birr for one bottle. I gave him a hundred-birr note to pay for this and future orders.

"How do you like this place?" said Asepha, leaning toward me.

"Very nice," I said. "These women are some of the most beautiful I have seen so far in Addis."

"True," said Asepha. "It is an exclusive bar managed like a club."

I sipped the sour potent drink. I can't say I liked it, but I made polite appreciative noises.

"Your English is good," I said to Asepha.

"I spent two years in an officers' course in Georgia. And I have news for you, sir. I was in a parachute course in Israel in 1971. I loved your country and my Israeli friends. Unfortunately, I have no more contact with them." He looked at me in a particularly receptive way.

"Perhaps you will have an opportunity to renew your acquaintance with Israel. I am here. Your ambassador is in Israel. Times are changing."

The girls kept trying to distract our conversation, using their limited English. "Where are you from?" "Which hotel you stay?" "Do you want more drinks?" The woman next to me had an infectious smile and penetrating eyes. More than her beauty, though, there was something in her manner—serene and ethereal—that was profoundly arresting. She made it hard for me to concentrate. I told her she could buy another drink. Then I turned to Asepha.

"I may have come at the wrong time in Ethiopia's history," I said. "I feel deeply about Ethiopia for obvious reasons."

"Yes. Your country and mine are alike. We are surrounded by Muslim neighbors who regard us as foreigners, in just the same way that they regard Israel. And we share Israel's spiritual and religious heritage."

"During the 1960s Israel extended more aid to Ethiopia than any other country."

"I know," said Asepha. "But we have always been wary of an adverse reaction from the Muslim world. So our appreciation has been expressed behind closed doors."

"Ben-Gurion wanted to develop relationships with 'periphery countries,' those just outside the ring of hostile countries that surrounded us. With that in mind, he focused on friendship with the Shah's Iran, Turkey, and Ethiopia."

"A wise policy," said Asepha.

"What about Deir-as-Sultan?" I asked. "This is another way we have been linked."

Asepha just nodded. Perhaps he had no interest in this controversy. For more than forty years, Israel has been involved in control over Deir-as-Sultan, an Ethiopian foothold on the roof of the Church of the Holy Sepulchre in Jerusalem (where Jesus is supposed to be entombed). A dozen Ethiopian monks live on the roof in primitive conditions, without sewage or electricity. The steps that lead off the roof to the church itself are behind a locked door, the keys to which are in the hands of the Egyptian monks who are stationed nearby. These monks refuse to open the door for the Ethiopians.

The struggle is recent. The Egyptian Coptic Church and the Ethiopian Orthodox Church have cooperated since time immemorial. They are both Monophysite Christians who believe in the single nature of Christ—a doctrine that dates from the Council of Chalcedon in 451. The Ethiopian church was an offshoot of the Coptic church, and the Copts traditionally appointed an Egyptian priest as the Abuna, or head of the Ethiopian church.

But in 1959, the Ethiopian church declared its independence from the Copts. Since then, its Abuna has been elected by Ethiopian bishops. The Copts were not happy about this; they retaliated by locking Deir-as-Sultan's door. The Ethiopian monks further retaliated by breaking the Copts' lock and installing their own, thus gaining control of the entrance to the church. The Egyptian monks asked the Israeli government to restore the status quo. Israel refused to interfere in the relations between religious groups, although we have tried to initiate compromises on both sides with little success.

ASEPHA, ON HIS fourth drink, was becoming emotional. Tadese took the woman with the pink dress for a dance, and, inwardly, I thanked him for it.

Asepha looked at me, considering. "Ethiopia may not be spared in this change. We've made a number of mistakes, and I'm not sure they can be corrected."

"You have the largest army in Africa," I said, drawing him out. "What are you afraid of?"

"You Israelis know better than anyone that quantity does not assure victory. There is more than arms to a battle."

"Yes, you need good military intelligence, a feeling of unity, and strong will to win, no matter what the odds."

It was ten, just two hours before curfew; the place was emptying. People were either returning home or going upstairs with women. The unattached girls seemed eager to depart. Many had a long walk ahead of them. Tadese, tactfully, took the girl in brown to the bartender. Asepha and I were left alone.

He sighed. "I'm afraid we have none of the things that you mentioned that are prerequisites to winning a war. This is not an invading army of a foreign country where we can unite against a common enemy who is endangering our way of life. Instead, this is a civil war—an internal rebellion between the Mengistu regime and the rebels from three major Ethiopian groups who want to change the government. It's not a war of life and death. Whoever wins, Ethiopia will survive with Eritrea as an independent state or an autonomous region. The soldiers find it difficult to get excited about the war. In many cases, they have to fight their own kind—Amhara against Amhara, Tigrenian against Tigrenian."

"But why are they fighting? Haven't both the government and the rebels adopted Marxist-Leninist ideology? Aren't both assisted by the USSR and other communist countries? How do they reconcile themselves and how does the USSR reconcile this fighting between their allies?"

Asepha laughed. "It's part of the paradox of Cold War politics. The Russians tried and failed to end the conflict. Now they figure they're winners whoever wins." He raised his glass and drank. His eyes were remarkably bright and clear for having drunk so much. His attention had stopped periodically wandering around the room to survey the sylphlike women in their seductive poses. He now seemed fixed on a vision of demise.

"The USSR is falling apart. Russian shipments of arms have stopped. Supplies to our soldiers on the front don't arrive on time and in sufficient quantity. So our units often take farmers' products without paying. They take their chickens. They mess with their daughters. The farmers, who are the backbone of the country, don't see the soldiers as protectors. They often fear them." His voice had filled with self-pity. "But the rebels are under strict orders to buy everything they need with cash and not to interfere with the farmers' work. They make friends wherever they go."

I felt that I had to interrupt this tale of woe. "I heard that mis-behavior by soldiers is sporadic and the army is trying to combat it."

"True. But in the background is the government policy of *kolhosisation*. Farmers were told to leave their homes and farms and move to a center village where all land was tilled as one unit, like the *kolhose* in the Soviet Union. The products were brought to market at the price set by the government, from which the farmers draw a salary. From the year the policy went into effect, the amount of grain produced by the farmers has steadily fallen. The government has finally decided to give back the farmers' plots. We are learning. But are we too late to change the trend?"

I showed sympathy and professed admiration for Asepha's expertise and understanding, probing deeper into the murky areas of Ethiopian politics. "The rebel forces, both the Eritrean Peoples Liberation Front that fights for independence from Ethiopia, and the Tigrean Peoples Liberation Front, which fights to depose Mengistu, have roughly a hundred thousand fighters. On the other hand, Ethiopia's army is estimated at three hundred thousand, with far superior equipment. Not to mention the fact that the Tigreans are only three million against the eighteen mil-lion Amhara that support the government. Also, there are gov-ernment offices all over the country. Why aren't these sources of high-grade intelligence?"

"Intelligence is only good when the army analyzes it and uses it in battle. That isn't happening."

"Still," I pressed, "the government forces are equipped with tanks, trucks, *katiushot*"—cluster bombs—"and an air force of MIGs. That should give you a big advantage."

Asepha answered in a cryptic way. "The government should do more. The morale of the population is as low as the morale of the army. Superior force cannot assure victory in an internal war. We are waging a war for the hearts of the people."

TADESE CAME BACK from dancing and showed me his watch. It read 11:25 P.M.—time to go before the midnight curfew. Asepha rose. For the first time I saw that he was short and plump. He was steady on his feet and his eyes were clear, even after all the drinks. I offered him a ride, but he said that he had a car.

Tadese asked me to drop him on Asmara road, close to his house. He leaned close to me as we drove through the sleeping city.

"My grandfather was Jewish," he said, almost in a whisper. "I want to go to Israel."

I felt uncomfortable and didn't know what to say. I knew from Zimna that many Ethiopians claim to have Jewish grandfathers or grandmothers in order to be able to take advantage of the Israeli Law of Return (which recognizes as a Jew anyone who has a Jewish grandfather or grandmother). Most Ethiopians were willing to do anything to emigrate to almost any other country.

I suddenly felt weary and sad. What an impossible place—war torn, poor beyond measure, without hope or future. Tadese seemed to be pleading. The Jeep rattled along. It was cold in Addis at night.

"I'll check into it with Zimna," I said.

Tadese nodded, not looking at me.

I thanked him, and we shook hands before I let him off in front of a hovel, a wispy curtain over its front door, on a street that was dead and black.

• • •

WHEN I CHECKED with Zimna, he just laughed. "Him, too," he said. "I never thought I'd live to see the day."

"What can you expect, Zimna? There's no future for him here. Nothing."

"That's true, Asher. I'm sorry. I didn't mean to be unfeeling."

After that night, it was never the same between us when Tadese came to give me lessons. The evening should have brought us closer, but, instead, it seemed that a shadow had been cast over our friendship.

FIFTEEN

ONIONS AND HERBS

"Ester has been asking after you," said Zimna, one morning when he had come to breakfast with me at the Hilton. "She wants you to visit the clinic."

I looked at my watch. I was already late to the embassy.

"Why not," I said on impulse. "Let's go."

Konata drove us. The clinic was located off the Asmara road, a mile or two closer to downtown than the Israeli embassy, just behind the traffic police headquarters. It was a brick house. Twenty or so people were waiting—coughing people, people with festering wounds, children so thin it looked as if their bones could shatter like glass.

The house was clean, freshly painted with new furniture and tiles on the floor. Dr. Rick Hodes, an American specialist in infectious diseases, was checking a baby who had suffered with diarrhea for a month, and Dr. Eli Schwartz, an Israeli with the same specialty, had just finished treating an elderly woman with a large open sore on her leg that was clearly infected.

"You must be kept very busy here with so many diseases," I said. "I know about them from the dozens of injections I had to take before flying here!"

"Yes," said Schwartz, gently cleaning the wound. "The diseases are dreadful: meningitis, yellow fever, polio, hepatitis B, diphtheria, and tetanus. Small children are the most vulnerable."

Hodes came over. "Before the clinic opened in the summer of 1990, there was a death rate of forty Falashas a month. Can you imagine?"

"Why was that?" I asked.

"No preparations had been made to receive them, house them, or feed them in Addis. We had a death rate of thirty in September, but this month it was down to thirteen."

"It wasn't easy to get the death rate down," said Schwartz. "The Falashas had no problems taking the food we provided and monthly stipends. But they refused free medicine because they were used to the traditional village healer, a witch doctor who cured with herbs, trance, and ritual to banish *zafar* [demons]. The Falashas see injections as punishment, and they don't believe in pills. So we have been sending nurses to Falasha homes, and we won't release their monthly payment without proof that they have been here."

Hodes excused himself. Schwartz continued. "First, we vaccinated the whole community against tuberculosis, the most common ailment. It's epidemic now in Africa and was spreading quickly in the cramped conditions of Addis. It needs six months of treatment to cure."

"Why does it take so long?"

"Antibiotics first kill the weaker bacteria and then the more resilient strains. But if the patient stops taking the medicine in the middle of treatment, because he starts to feel better, the stronger bacteria develop resistance, and the disease becomes difficult to cure."

I hesitated to bring it up, but I felt that I had to. "What about the AIDS situation?" I said. "I heard that Ethiopians believe HIV is curable by traditional healers with an onion and herbs."

Schwartz sighed. "Unfortunately, that's true. The Beta Israel probably didn't have AIDS in their villages. They lived in a traditional, conservative, family-oriented society—far from the city with its bars and brothels."

"Is it true that many Beta Israel men are sampling Addis's nightlife?"

"What do you expect? They're idle, without work. They have money from JDC, and the red-light districts draw them. And they become infected with HIV."

I suddenly felt afraid. "How big is the problem?"

Schwartz looked at me closely. "You haven't heard what happened in Jerusalem?"

"No!"

"We started testing for HIV here and found a 1 percent rate of infection in the Falasha population. Our findings got back to Jerusalem."

"What happened?"

"A government official panicked, and convened a meeting to discuss a proposal to refuse immigration visas to Falashas who tested positive for HIV."

"What office was this?"

"I think it was the Ministry of Health, but I'm not sure. At any rate, at the meeting, there was a broad spectrum of people—social workers and attorneys as well as bureaucrats. The proposal was shot down as discriminatory. Will American Jews have to pass AIDS tests to make *aliyah*?"

SCHWARTZ LEFT TO attend a child with high fever. Zimna and Ester came in from the back of the place. Her face lit up when she saw me.

"Come, come," she said. "I want you to meet someone." I needed to digest Schwartz's news. Keeping the Beta Israel in Addis was, obviously, a riskier proposition than I had originally thought. Looking around the clinic at the sick, impoverished people, their eyes on the floor, I felt a great weariness.

Ester refused to let me brood. She was all activity and light. In her presence, I felt myself lighten, too. She took us to an adjacent room and introduced me to Menasse Meharto, whom Zimna already knew. He was a fragile-looking Ethiopian, small and slight, with a trimmed mustache and glasses. He wore a medical gown over a yellow shirt and brown pants. Ester explained that he had been hired as a general practitioner at the clinic after training in Israel. Menasse greeted me by bowing and taking my hand in both of his.

"Asher," said Ester, "I wanted you to meet Menasse because he has a close relationship with the *Kes* of *Kes*."

"Who is that?"

"The highest person in the religion," said Ester. "Like the chief rabbi."

"What exactly is a *kes*?" I asked.

"His role is ancient," said Menasse. "More than two millennia old. He's both our religious and community leader."

Ester challenged him: "You're saying the Beta Israel have been around since when, exactly?"

Menasse seemed startled that a woman was pushing him.

"Since 722 BCE," he finally said. "When the ten tribes of Israel were in exile. My ancestors went to Kush on the upper Nile."

Ester scoffed. "What proof do you have that we originated from these tribes? Are you relying on the Eldad ha-Dani legend?"

"That is no legend!" He was on the verge of real anger.

"What is the story of ha-Dani?" I asked. I felt that I had to interject.

"Let's go outside," said Ester, "if we're going to hear about the great ha-Dani."

Menasse took us out behind the building to a concrete patio set up with a table and chair. A deep ravine opened up beyond a field where gaunt cattle grazed and people walked, stately and slender, many barefoot, some in rags, a few carrying umbrellas to shade them from the sun. A steep river ran through the ravine, strewn with boulders. The river would have been beautiful except its bed was littered with trash. A woman was washing clothes on the rocks in one of its pools. Beyond the river was a shantytown. The makeshift homes were made of scraps of tin and cardboard. I looked up. In the sky, high above us, dozens of black birds were circling.

"What are those birds?" I asked Zimna.

"Vultures."

"What do they eat?"

He just looked at me.

Ester came out with bottled water and glasses. The morning sun was strong, and I was glad we were in the shade. I knew Houdek and probably Jerusalem were trying to get ahold of me at the embassy. But I felt an inability to move. I just wanted to sit.

Zimna read my mood and looked concerned, but Menasse plunged on, oblivious. "Eldad ha-Dani was a ninth-century Arabian Jew—a famous traveler. He wrote about his encounters with Jewish communities all over the Middle East. But his most amazing story relates to the Jews of Ethiopia. As you know, after King Solomon's death, Palestine was split in two, both sides warring against each other. According to ha-Dani, the tribe of Dan refused to go to war against their brothers in Judea, and instead decided to settle elsewhere. They eventually reached the head of the Nile in Ethiopia and settled here."

Ester interrupted him again. "But Menasse, scholars generally don't credit the ha-Dani story."

"Don't you believe in the Bible?" Menasse retorted. "The prophet Isaiah, chapter eighteen, explicitly mentions Kush." Menasse went inside and emerged with a Bible in his hand. He read:

> O land of buzzing wings,
> which fly beyond the river of Kush,
> Go swift messengers,
> to a nation far and remote,
> To a people thrust forth and away,
> A nation of gibber and chatter
> Whose land is cut off by streams;
> Which sends out envoys by sea, in papyrus upon the
>   waters.
> At the place where the name of the Lord of Hosts
>   abides,
> At Mount Zion.

"And it's prophesied that Ethiopian Jews will return to Israel. God through his prophets promised to gather 'His people,' Beta Israel included." He read again. "And it shall come to pass in the day, that the Lord shall set His Hand again the second time to recover the remnant of His people that shall be left from Assyria, and from Egypt, and from Parthos and from Kush and from

Elam, and from Shinar, and from Hamath, and from the islands of the sea. . . ."

Menasse ended the quote in triumph, and Ester and I clapped.

"Well, if it's in the Bible, who can argue?" I said to Ester.

"Bible or no Bible, it's all myth," she said, not giving an inch. She really had become a splendid Israeli.

The line of patients in the clinic had grown and Menasse had to attend to them.

"Zimna," said Menasse before we left. "Take Asher to see the *Kes* of *Kes*. Then he will understand who we are."

Zimna and I walked out to the car. Konata was polishing it with his ever-present chamois. His black suit was shiny, like an undertaker's. He could have been an undertaker except he wore no socks. Onions and herbs. I felt a surge of anger at Mengistu and his cronies. Kasa himself had told me that he knew that it was wrong for the Beta Israel to stay in Addis. Overhead the vultures circled. The sun was bright.

SIXTEEN

THE *KES* OF *KES*

The *Kes* of *Kes* was staying on the sixth floor of a concrete building near the center of downtown. We entered a dim, grimy lobby. Zimna pressed a button for an elevator, and, amazingly, we heard engines start. Lo and behold, the door opened and there it was. It was very dark inside. Zimna lit a match and pressed "6" and up we went.

The wife of the *Kes* of *Kes* opened the door to the one-room apartment. She was an old woman, her face seamed, her hair, still black, covered by a kerchief. She wore a long white *shammas*, belted at the waist with a sash. The *kes* rose to greet us. I bowed out of respect. He gave me a big smile and held my hand in both of his.

"*Tannestellin*," he said. God bless you and give you health.

Kes Hadana had a long bushy beard and mustache the color of snow. His face was thin, full of sensitivity and feeling. He had an aquiline nose. His soulful black eyes were planted deep in cavernous sockets. He wore a white tarboosh—a tight cloth cap—on his head. A loose white *shammas* covered him from his neck to his knees. Under it, I could see that he wore a gray jacket and white pantaloons. On his feet were dusty brown shoes without backs. He held a whisk in his right hand made from horsehair; with elegant flicks of his wrists, he dispersed the flies. I thought it was a practical implement, but Zimna said it was a sign of status.

Zimna translated. "Have you come from Jerusalem?" the *kes* asked.

When I told him I lived in the city, he closed his eyes and bent his forehead over our clasped hands.

There was a long moment of silence. He was very still. Finally he rose and looked at me; his eyes were deep, burning, and in them was a compassion and wisdom that I associate with some of our rabbis. "I hope to be in the holy city soon with all my people," Zimna translated.

"I am sure that will happen." As I said it I felt it was so. "That is why I am here."

WE SAT AROUND a small table. Mrs. Hadana made coffee on a small terrace above the din of the street, placing a ceramic pot with a long, gracefully curved spout on a bed of coals.

My meeting with the *kes* turned out to be a secondary purpose of the visit. The *kes* had summoned us to demand that we build a *masged*, a synagogue, in the embassy compound, to function as the center of communal life, as it had in Beta Israel villages. The *kes* saw this as a matter of some urgency, because there was beginning to be a looseness among the young men in the community. I immediately agreed to give up the garden to the south of my office to this project.

"Thanks, Asher," said Zimna. "It's done."

The *masged* would also serve as a meeting place for the *kessim*. *Kes* Hadana was pleased with such a quick response. The tension on his face faded and he asked his wife to pour us a second *bunna*.

I asked Zimna if the *kes* would discuss his view of the origin of Beta Israel. The *kes* bowed his head in assent. "My knowledge of this," he said, "was given to me by my father, also a *kes*. And it was given to him by his father before him. It's not in books. It's a spoken thing."

He flicked his whisk in front of his face, and coughed, a rasping sound deep in his chest. He inhaled sharply and his fine nostrils flared. His dark skin took on an ashen hue, and I wondered how old he was and how much longer he had to live . . . and who, if anyone, would replace him.

"I must admit that there are other versions in other parts of Ethiopia," he continued when he had recomposed himself. "Although about the basic story—that we have been here since ancient times—there is no dispute."

He told me that after the destruction of the First Temple in 586 BCE, most Israelites were exiled to Babylon. For the small group that was allowed to stay, the Babylonians appointed Gedaliah as governor. The people hated Gedaliah because he cooperated with the conquerors, and he was assassinated. Fearing Babylon's wrath, three hundred leaders of the community escaped to Egypt. They settled in the cities of Tafnes, Memphis, Migdal, and Patros, but their community center was on the Nile's Elephantine Island, near Aswan, where they built a luxurious synagogue modeled on the Temple in Jerusalem.

There they sacrificed and worshiped and kept the commandments for 450 years until the priests of the community, Elazar and Onn, differed. Onn wanted to continue the tradition of sacrifice while Elazar opposed it, arguing that it should be practiced in the

Temple in Jerusalem and nowhere else. When Onn insisted that the practice continue, Elazar tore his clothes as a sign of mourning and left Elephantine with part of the community, southward along the Nile.

The rest of the community stayed with Priest Onn, but after he died, the Egyptians persecuted them and they fled to Alexandria. They were persecuted there, too, so they fled south to Daftara, a village near the Ethiopian border, and stayed there for twenty years. In Daftara, they had a queen named Hannah. They were attacked, Hannah died, and the group went farther south to Kuwara.

Meanwhile, the first group headed by Elazar crossed the River Takezy in northern Ethiopia near the Red Sea. They were looking for Jewish women, and they heard the first group had moved to Chega in Gondar, where the community had built many synagogues.

I did not interrupt the *kes* through this fascinating if confusing tale. The correctness of the details wasn't important—its meaning and message were clear to me. The *kes* was trying to convey a simple message: "We are good Jews with a pedigree from high-class Israelites."

I ASKED THE *kes* how Beta Israel's Judaism differed from that in the rest of the Jewish world.

"Have you heard about our Jewish customs?" he asked.

"I have heard a little bit, but I would be honored if you would tell me more."

The *kes* bent forward, counting with his fingers. "We believe in the God of Israel, the absolute oneness of God, and that the Jews are God's chosen people on the basis of the law given on Mount

Sinai. We believe in reward and punishment, the afterworld, heaven and hell, resurrection of the dead, and the coming of the Messiah—in our case, he is known as Teodros—the return to Zion, and the ingathering of the exiles."

He had counted ten fingers for the ten points he had made.

I could see Zimna was following the *kes*'s story with reverence. Mrs. Hadana appeared with bananas and apples. I took a banana. The *kes* continued. "There are differences in our Judaism from other Jews. The Mishnah, Talmud, and other rabbinical literature never reached us. We were isolated. The Jewish world outside Ethiopia didn't know we existed. And we were not aware of the existence of other Jews."

Zimna was looking at me closely to read how the *kes*'s words affected me.

"What about these differences?" I asked. "What are they?"

"There are things you do that we don't do and vice versa," said the *kes*. "We don't do *mitzvoth* [commandments] such as *tzizit*, *tefilin*, *kippa* [the covering of the head in the synagogue in particular], and the hanging of the *mazuza* at the doors. We don't celebrate bar mitzvah. We fast and have *ta'anit Ester* [the fast that precedes Purim], but we do not celebrate Purim or Hanukkah or the other holidays instituted after the destruction of the Temple."

His voice sounded almost sheepish, as though he was telling me not to blame him for those omissions.

"Please tell him I understand perfectly and not to be reserved," I said to Zimna.

"On the other hand," the *kes* continued, "we do observe the holidays prescribed in the Torah, although our calendar is often different from the rabbinical calendar. We celebrate Rosh Hashanah, the New Year. We call it *Berhan Saraka*—the rising light. On Yom Kippur, we fast. Succoth is called *Baìala Masalat*—festival of the shade. It is an eight-day harvest festival, and a portion of the crop is offered to the *kessim*. We don't build a *sukkah* [hut]. On Passover, we fast the first day and in the evening we sacrifice. The following day is a holiday, followed by seven days of eating unleavened bread."

I was deeply moved. "It's amazing to me," I said, "that you have kept all this alive through the centuries!"

"Thank you, Asher," said Zimna. "I want to add that throughout our history we were under pressure or threat to convert to Christianity, sometimes under penalty of death. But there were also conversions of Christians to Judaism." Zimna leaned forward and his eyes were on me. "And this, Asher, I'm sure will be of particular interest to you. In the fifteenth century, Abba Sabrah— a Christian aristocrat who converted to Judaism—began the practice of Nazarenes, or Jewish monks. The monks lived in isolated *tukuls* for many years, praying and studying the holy writings and making sure to avoid any contact with people or unclean animals, which would cause ritual impurity. These monks were considered saints."

The *kes* nodded. "It is total devotion to God," he said.

"Jewish monks," I said. "You're kidding me! I've never heard of such a thing."

"Well," said Zimna, pleased, "now you have."

"Can I meet one?"

"Perhaps," said the *kes*.

MRS. HADANA CAME in with coffee. We sat sipping. I was full of questions, but I felt the *kes* tiring. He had coughed throughout our conversation, and his face was gray.

"Let's go," I said to Zimna. "I can tell he's tired."

I rose but the *kes* spoke sharply to Zimna. "He says you must have coffee. And he can see that you still have questions."

"But he is tired. And we've taken so much of his time. We can come another day."

Zimna translated. The *kes* coughed, recovered, and then replied.

"Not another day," said Zimna. "Today. He says it is important that you finish with your questions."

I sighed and sat.

"Okay," I said. "What role does the *kes* play in the community?"

"We keep the calendar and declare the dates of the Jewish holidays," the *kes* replied. "We are scattered through hundreds of villages. We make sure that each belongs to a *masged*, which is built according to our tradition. We conduct all the religious affairs of the community and teach the Torah and its commandments. In turn, members of the community provide gifts and donations from their harvests and possessions. We serve as judges in disputes, together with the *shmagla*"—the elders.

"How does one become a *kes*?" I asked.

Again there was silence as the *kes* coughed and hung his head.

"We really should go," I told Zimna.

"Hush," said Zimna and there was sharpness in his voice. "Listen."

The *kes* cleared his throat and composed himself. "The title of *kes* is awarded after studies and examinations," he resumed. "This finishes with ordination by the other *kessim*. A *kes* must lead a clean family life. He must set an example with his behavior. A divorced person can't be a *kes*."

"What about women? Can a women become a *kes*?"

Zimna translated. The *Kes* of *Kes* threw back his head and laughed. "Now you can go," he said.

I got up and thanked him. Zimna repeated his promise to start building the *masged* immediately. We thanked Mrs. Hadana and went down the dark elevator and out onto the street.

• • •

I TOLD ZIMNA how impressed I was with *Kes* Hadana's explanations.

"Asher," said Zimna in his serious way, "you must tell the rabbis to have more compassion in the way they approach the *kessim.*"

"*Oy!* They give the *kessim tsorris,* too?"

"Of course! What do you think!"

Our Jeep was stopped at Ras Mekonin Avenue at the entrance to Abiot Square as an argument ensued about the price to be paid for the sheep that had been killed by a motorist. The street was wide, with easily enough room to drive a couple of trucks around the incident, but with a great show of self-importance the police had blocked off the entire road, stopping traffic, standing with their hands on their holsters. I proposed that we park and go to the Bahar-Dar Salon on the corner of the square.

The place was crowded, and foggy with cigarette smoke. All the tables were occupied. Most of the customers were young. The atmosphere was subdued and genteel. Some of the girls were stunning in their beauty. Beautiful young people are accidents of nature, but beautiful old people are works of art. I thought of the *kes* and his deep, soulful eyes.

When the waitress saw us, she immediately found volunteers to empty a table for a *faranji* (foreigner). We ordered *bunna,* three birr, and the waitress beamed with thanks when I gave her a ten-birr note and told her to keep it.

"Now tell me exactly what is the story with the rabbis and the *kessim,*" I said to Zimna.

"The good part is that it is doable and fixable," said Zimna. "The bad part is that our hearts are bleeding, not only from *what* they ask from us, but the *way* they do it."

109

I asked Zimna to please make me understand the problem and what was behind it.

"The rabbis have robbed the *kessim* of their souls, their standing in their community, their pride, and the only thing they know and are trained to do. The rabbis told them they can't be recognized as rabbis and they have their own reasons, namely that *kessim* don't know the *halacha*."

Zimna stopped and looked at me.

"Zimna, I know what *halacha* is," I said when it was clear he wasn't going to continue. "It's the legal side of Judaism, particularly rabbinical writings on personal, social, and political relationships, and all other practices and observances of Judaism."

Just by saying this I already could see the difficulties. If, as they themselves admit, the *kessim* practice a pre-Talmudic Judaism, it is clear that they don't know the very complex legal rulings that took two thousand years to evolve. Beta Israel were not part of this modification of Jewish thought and practice.

"Will the *kessim* agree to attend rabbinical seminars and to be reordained under current Jewish practices?" I asked.

"Rabbinical seminars for the *kessim* are impractical because of their age and lack of Hebrew. For younger *kessim*, maybe it is a solution."

"Then where is the problem?"

Zimna called the waitress to remove the dishes and asked me if he could order beer.

"Of course," I replied.

The waitress brought Pilsner, a locally brewed beer.

Zimna smiled and emptied the bottle in a long gulp.

"The refusal to recognize the *kes* as rabbis is insulting to the whole community."

I felt for Zimna, but what could I say? I knew the rabbis. They would never accept the *kessim* in their ranks.

The road had cleared. When we left the restaurant, Zimna put his arm around my shoulder, a sign of brotherhood. I had similar feelings. Personally, my attitude toward any Jew is the same. Orthodox, Conservative, Reform, or Beta Israel. Being Jewish is by choice, and we have suffered for that choice in each generation. Why then should we inflict pain on our own brothers?

"Tomorrow," Zimna said, "we will start building the synagogue. You know, it's constructed just like the Temple in Jerusalem."

I suddenly had an image of a huge, looming structure sprawling over the embassy grounds.

"What have we done, Zimna?"

"In miniature, of course," he laughed.

And the next day I did watch the structure begin to take form. It took only a couple of days to build. Many people worked on it. There was great joy in its building. It was a large *tukul*, with a thatched grass roof and mud and sticks for walls.

The *Kes* of *Kes* came to supervise its building, and I watched the way the people deferred to him and kissed his hands and looked at him with love. He was very weak. He walked slowly with a stooped gait, flicking his whisk, and I found myself offering a silent prayer that he would live to see the holy city.

The *masged's* name derived from the word in Ge'ez for "to bow." Everyone bowed when entering the *masged*. It was divided into two parts, just like the Temple in Jerusalem, with an inner sanctum, the *Kadesta Kedushan* (reminiscent of the Hebrew *Kodesh Hakodashim*—the Holy of Holies) where the Orit (the Torah) was kept. Worshipers removed their shoes before entering. The floor was packed earth. Men came to services. Old women and children were allowed in a special section, while young women stayed in a separate place or outside the *tukul*.

It was a pleasure to see all this take shape from my office window. But there was also a poignancy about it. I had the feeling I was witnessing the end of something. I thought of the exacting standards of the rabbis. And I knew that I couldn't protect the ardent congregants from what was sure to be a fearful and for some impossible leap from their ancient ways to modern Judaism. Again, I was forced to wonder what was in store for them in the land of milk and honey.

SEVENTEEN

GORAD GORAD

Kasa summoned me; I had no idea about what. When I arrived, he was all smiles.

"Asher," he said. "You have been minister of information at the Israeli embassy in Washington. That makes you an expert on public relations, at least as far as the United States is concerned. I need your help."

"Sure, Kasa," I said. After the Shitrit affair I was more than willing to appease him in any way I could.

"Can you join me for dinner tonight at my house? Two public relations people from Washington will be there."

"I would be delighted."

"Wonderful. My driver will pick you up at nine."

AT NINE, I went to the hotel lobby. An Ethiopian came over to me, bowed, and showed me car keys, indicating that he was Kasa's driver. I followed him to a shining Mercedes with dark leather upholstery. I lost track of direction as we traversed a warren of unpaved residential streets with walled one-story buildings to either side. A large gate swung open, letting the car into an open, rather neglected parking lot.

Two male servants appeared, ushering me to the front door where I was met by Mrs. Kasa—a very pretty, elegantly dressed woman in her early forties. I knew from Lubrani that she had her own career at the United Nations office in Geneva. Kasa had been the Ethiopian ambassador to Switzerland for five years, trying to win the rebels back to the Addis government, but he'd failed because he'd offered too little, too late.

Mrs. Kasa led me inside. A waiter brought me a drink. The house had a large living room, its floors covered, wall to wall, with straw mats overlaid with carpets. Embroidered tapestries hung on the walls. European and Ethiopian chairs (upholstered in animal skins) were scattered throughout. The mahogany coffee table was pushed to a corner, leaving more space for sitting on the floor. Off the living room was a study, furnished with a French-style desk, a mahogany chair, filing cabinet, telephone, and fax. The other rooms were closed, but through a glass door I could see steps leading to the second floor, all built in wood. The trim garden was dimly lit, revealing a small pool and sun umbrella.

It was clear that the lifestyle of upper echelon Ethiopians was opulent, particularly when compared to the wretched poverty of the majority of the population. The contrast reminded me of the mid–nineteenth century Yiddish writer Shalom Aleichem, who identified with the poor, depicting the humor, wisdom, humiliation, pride, and poverty of the Jewish Pale in Ukraine. He is known in the West for his hero Tevye in the story "Fiddler on the Roof," who said, "Life is a dream for the wise, a game for the fool, a comedy for the rich, a tragedy for the poor." Was it a dream or a comedy for Kasa?

He wore a gray suit, and a belt over his bulging belly. He introduced me to Jean and Charlie from Washington—she in her late thirties, he, a decade older—both conservatively dressed with a hard businesslike air about them. Kasa did not tell me their surnames or the name of their company. I immediately felt they were uneasy about my presence: A deal was in the works that they didn't want disrupted.

We sat on floor cushions. I could smell the straw, sweet and grassy, from the mats beneath me. It was as though the savanna had been brought into the house. Two servants appeared with a large skewer. Mounted on it was a slab of raw bloody beef. They set the skewer on a plastic mat close to Kasa. A large copper platter contained dipping bowls, vegetables, condiments and *injera*.

"*Gorad gorad!*" said Kasa with delight as he shaved pieces of bloodred flesh from the skewer. "Just slaughtered. It's the only way to eat meat." I didn't know what to say. The sight alone made me gag. I had seen how Ethiopian butcher shops in town hung similar skewers in the open, in a haze of exhaust, dust, and flies. This was a cleaner atmosphere, but I couldn't help visualizing the shops.

Kasa cut meat. Jean talked on about the house she had bought on Connecticut Avenue in Washington, and the climbing price of the city's real estate. Charlie criticized the leftist views of the *Washington Post*. Kasa served the meat to each of us in turn, showing us how to dip it into bowls of a very hot red pepper sauce.

As a diplomat, there had been many occasions on which a local host had served food that was not to my liking. I had developed a system, taking very little of the main dish and filling my plate with bread and vegetables. But at Kasa's there was only meat and *injera*, and he was personally filling my plate.

I managed to put the first piece of raw meat in the corner of my plate and covered it with a piece of *injera*. But Kasa, smart guy, read my intentions. He kept looking at me and following my actions. I tried to keep busy talking, but Kasa didn't relent and continued looking at me. Then I came up with a brilliant idea.

"Kasa, I keep kosher and don't eat raw meat," I said. He knew that this was an excuse, but he was a good host and tried to please me. He ordered the meat cooked in sauce, which was hot but tasty. Jean and Charlie eyed my plate enviously. Kasa succumbed and we were all served the cooked meat.

TOWARD THE END of the meal Kasa turned to me. "Asher," he said, "Ethiopia's representative in Washington hides. He does nothing! I personally suspect that he sympathizes with the rebels. So, on my last visit to the States, I hired the companies that these two people represent to give us a positive image in the international media. What do you think?"

I saw Jean and Charlie lean toward us with hard suspicious looks.

"PR people can't create something from nothing," I said.

"You know that we have started a policy of privatization with the farmers."

"That's good, but not enough. The world wants to see food from humanitarian organizations delivered across the rebel lines to starving women and children. No PR company can change the use of famine victims as an instrument of war."

Kasa spread his hands in a placating gesture. "We are progressing step by step. One can't expect total change at once."

"One thing that can gain goodwill for Ethiopia immediately is to let a large group of Falashas leave for Israel. Do that and you will do more for Ethiopia than any number of PR companies."

Kasa leaned back, eyes half closed. "Falashas and more Falashas," he said. "That's all you care about." His eyes grew hard. "You are ungrateful. Thousands of Falashas have left. We have made great progress in the family unification program. But always you Israelis are impatient. You yell and scream."

I had to back off. "Listen, Kasa. All I'm saying is the change in policy has to be real. America is asking for three things." I ticked them off on my fingers. "Willingness to negotiate with the rebels. Allowing humanitarian aid to starving Ethiopians in the north. And free emigration of Falashas to Israel. If you do these things sincerely, even partially, these PR people can be of great help."

Kasa was about to respond when he was called to the phone. A few minutes later, he reappeared, seeming pensive and distracted. He asked me to arrange a meeting for him with Lubrani in Israel.

"I'm going to Cuba, maybe to Moscow and Albania, too. I will make a stopover in Israel. We need help now!"

IT WAS ALREADY late, curfew time, when I left. Kasa called a police car to escort me back to the Hilton. Jean and Charlie were staying there, too, but they did not accompany me. Their goodbyes were chilly.

Outside Kasa's gates was a different world. Spectral dogs rummaged in the gutters. Beggars huddled against the walls, wrapped in thin cloaks. The Mercedes wove slowly through the pitted streets, its engine quietly purring. The government espoused an egalitarian philosophy. Yet here in Ethiopia, as in other so-called communist societies around the world, all people were not equal.

The country's leaders lacked nothing. They ate in the best restaurants, imported all they needed, and traveled abroad at will.

Professor Binyamin Aktzin, a professor of political science at Hebrew University, once asked my class, "Does anyone have a definition of what a revolution is?" The students offered ideological answers. Aktzin smiled. "My dear students," he said, "in a revolution the class that ruled is replaced by those who have been ruled. Very little else is changed."

In Ethiopia's case, that definition exactly fit. Absolute rulers have always reigned in Ethiopia, and land was traditionally the source of their wealth, status, and power.

From time immemorial, control of Ethiopia's land and its wealth had belonged to the emperor. He distributed land, together with its inhabitants, to trusted generals and vassals. When vassals died, their holdings reverted to the crown, which decided whether to allow its transfer to the vassal's heirs.

Peasants who worked the land were tenant farmers and had to pay about half of their produce to the absentee landlords. The tenant farmers owed fealty to feudal lords, but they still owned their little plots of land.

In the modern era, it was clear that Ethiopia desperately needed land reform. Agrarian reform was discussed in the National Assembly, which was first convened in 1957. As in czarist Russia and imperial Iran, Ethiopia's feudal landowners opposed change. The emperor could, of course, have overruled them and imposed agrarian reform, but he preferred to prevent confrontation.

The revolution had changed things, but Aktzin's definition held true. Although Mengistu's regime had nationalized most land and created Russian-style *kolhoses*, the farmers were actually worse off than they had been under the imperial system.

The Jews of Ethiopia were of even a lower status than the tenant farmers. They were deprived of landownership because they were Jews, just like the Jews of Europe in the Middle Ages. Instead, they were loaned land by vassal lords. Since land was the source of wealth and status, the Ethiopian Jews lacked both.

To supplement their income, the Jews had developed other professions. They became weavers, potters, and ironworkers, engaging in work that their Amharic neighbors abhorred. They were also believed to possess the *buda*, the evil eye, a superstition common throughout Africa. They were regularly persecuted for bringing sickness and death to their Christian neighbors. Some Ethiopians believed that Falashas changed at night into man-hunting animals, such as lions or hyenas.

How strange, I thought, that the same demonizing of Jews existed here in the heart of Africa that bedeviled Jews in other areas of the world. Why? Because we are different? Because we are a minority, easy to blame for all calamities? Because in many societies we have distinguished ourselves and provoked envy?

The roads of Addis were completely empty. No one stopped us. It was an eerie ride back to the Hilton. As the crossing bar was lifted at the Hilton's gate, and I again entered its enclave of privilege, I had an odd feeling of having moved between two insulated worlds—Kasa's house and the hotel—in the buffered cocoon of the car. I was suddenly sick of Addis, its dizzying disparities of wealth, its curfew, its prostitutes and beggars, its corrupt politicians grasping at power. Schmoozing Kasa was part of my job, but it had left a bad taste in my mouth.

The guards were sleeping and jumped groggily to attention when my key rattled in the lock. David must have heard me come in: He knocked when I was just inside my door. "Where have you been?" he said, an edge to his voice.

"Never mind. Listen, we're leaving. I want to get out of the city and see the Falasha villages. I need a change of scene. Let's leave as soon as possible. We'll take Zimna and two Jeeps from the embassy."

PART TWO

OPERATION
SOLOMON

EIGHTEEN

SAFARI

Air streamed in through the open windows. Our convoy of Jeeps blazed up a long stretch of gently rising road, the tumbling hovels and filthy concrete storefronts of Addis's northern outskirts whizzing past and then dropping away behind us. We were climbing, the steep wall of mountain rising up, the cool early-morning air spiced with eucalyptus.

People flowed into the city from the hills. Many of the women were weighed down by huge sheaves of sticks on their backs. They were dressed in smocklike frocks of unbleached cotton, bound at the waist with a white sash. They walked barefoot with a bent-kneed, bouncing gait that propelled them forward, so they seemed to be running.

"So poor," said Zimna.

"What do they carry?" I asked.

"Firewood."

"For cooking or heat?"

Zimna laughed. "Heat! In Ethiopia no one knows about heat."

"But it's cold in Addis at night."

"Don't worry, Asher. Where we're going it's warmer."

Zimna was particularly excited that our trip to the north coincided with the *Seged*, an ancient Beta Israel ritual found nowhere else in the Jewish world.

"It is particularly auspicious that we're going to participate," Zimna had said. "This may be the last *Seged* in Ethiopia."

We passed a dump truck loaded with stones. There was a bump in the road and the truck bucked, sending a few small boulders bouncing toward us. Zimna braked, just missing a stone the size of a pumpkin, which flew past my window, crashing into the forest, splintering trees. Zimna brought the Jeep to a full stop in the middle of the road. I looked back to see David's Jeep pulled over, the truck careening around a turn, black smoke spewing from its tailpipe.

David came running up along with Kasahoon, an aide at the embassy, an army veteran who worked with Ethiopian army intelligence and whom we had brought along for his great knowledge of the highland people.

After they had ascertained that we were uninjured, we started out again. We came up over a saddle in the mountain, very high now. The city was spread out below us. A strong wind rolled over the pass. Our two Jeeps were fully loaded with five jerry cans of gasoline, three water containers, and a five-day supply of food, consisting mainly of sandwiches and fruit.

We dropped down off the mountain onto a broad grassy plateau, much of it in crops, the sun now well up, the Jeep bouncing along nicely.

"*Teff*," said Zimna, pointing at vivid bright swaths of slender grass, perhaps twelve to eighteen inches tall. The *teff* seemed to glow with an almost hallucinogenic potency.

"What's that?" I asked of grain that was a darker green, thicker, and more loosely spaced.

"Barley."

Big mountains loomed in the distance. It was if we had slipped back in time, the city forgotten. A farmer plowed a field with a bull. When we came closer, we were surprised to discover that the farmer was a young boy, wearing a shirt that barely came to his knees and nothing else.

David, who was in an exuberant mood and knew some Amharic, stopped to talk to him. The child abandoned his plowing and moved away. David ran to the car and brought some biscuits. Still the child hesitated. Kasahoon interceded and engaged him. Only then did he come forward, his face and arms caked with dirt. Flies, unnoticed, attached to the corners of his eyes and mouth. My heart filled with pity. Kasahoon spoke to him softly. He finally reached out and took our offering.

"Maybe you are the first white men he has seen," said Zimna.

As we drove away he was still standing where we had left him. We waved but he just stared at us blankly, holding the biscuit.

FARTHER ALONG THE foot traffic became heavy. Zimna explained that we were approaching a town and it was a market day. We saw many donkeys, in groups of ten or more, each loaded with saddlebags of *teff*. Herds of goats and sheep trotted by the roadside, tails twitching. David, ahead of us, stopped again. He and Kasahoon quickly became embroiled in a discussion with the goatherd.

"Hey, Ambassador," David said. "How much will you give for a goat?"

"You want a goat?"

"Of course. We'll eat it tonight!"

I loved this idea.

"Okay!" I clapped my hands. "How many birr?" I said to the goatherd.

He was a young man, bearded, barefoot, with a thin nose and a shepherd's staff resting on his thin shoulder. He turned to Kasahoon, and they gently conferred, none of the heated haggling that accompanies any transaction in the Middle East. David and I couldn't stand this civility and we inserted ourselves, trying to make it a melee.

Our cries of "how many birr?" eventually drew smiles from the herder. I noticed, as in the case of the young plower, that Zimna kept his distance.

"One hundred birr," I called out.

"He says 180 birr," Kasahoon said. "This is *faranji* price. If I were alone it would be priced at one hundred birr."

I launched into negotiations with renewed vigor.

Zimna, who had been following all this silently, took me aside. "Asher," he said. "If you really want a goat we'll get one in Gondar. I don't think we want to carry it."

I was deflated. "Yes, yes. You're right, of course."

"Give him ten birr," I said to Kasahoon. "All this back-and-forth. I don't want to leave him with nothing."

I called David off, and we piled back into the Jeeps.

KASAHOON WENT WITH me, and David with Zimna. The farther we were from Addis, the more breathtaking the scenery became. It reminded me of the American West—the canyonlands of Arizona, New Mexico, and Utah. Mountains rose sharply from the plateau, steep and serrated, their slopes highly eroded, flecked with green trees, a dizzying conglomeration of mesas and buttes.

The mountains were dry, banded with yellows and browns, while the rolling plateau we traveled on was patched with crops.

We passed a man in his fifties riding a horse. He held a colorful umbrella over his head and wore colorful clothing.

"This is the head of the village," said Kasahoon, "heading for the market or possibly to a neighbor to ask for a partner in marriage for one of his sons." He laughed, proud of his explanation.

The whole scene was pleasantly pastoral, far removed from the Addis tension, if one could only ignore the poverty behind it.

We lunched in a valley, near a small waterfall. David and Kasahoon cleared an area, set up a "table" on stones, and opened the lunchboxes. A dozen or so people appeared from all sides.

"Where do they come from?" I asked Kasahoon.

"We say the mountains have 'eyes.' We are being constantly watched by people. Some are armed and paid by the government to look for *shifta* or rebel groups. This country has always had rebels." He kicked the earth with his boot.

We distributed sandwiches, pens (which seemed to be in high demand), birr, and drove on to Bahar-Dar, meaning "gate to the sea," a small city set on Lake Tana, an enormous body of water that was the source of the Blue Nile.

Outside Bahar-Dar, the road skirted the Nile. We looked down to a blue-green sluice of river, a couple of hundred yards wide. There were green fields on either side and verdurous slopes of cypress, palm, and flowering trees.

"In Ethiopia we call the Nile the Abbay River," said Kasahoon.

"A pretty name," I replied. "I've heard that none of the Nile's water stays in Ethiopia."

"That is Ethiopia's tragedy. Twenty-five percent of our water goes to Sudan, the other 75 percent to Egypt." His voice was angry. "The Abbay supplies 82 percent of the Nile's water. The other 18 percent comes from the White Nile in Uganda. The rivers meet in Khartoum, Sudan's capital. The Abbay carries tons of silt that enriches Egypt's farmland."

"That's why Egypt likes to 'stir the pot' in Ethiopian affairs. They want Ethiopia at war with itself with no time for major development that may require Nile water. Now, too, the Arabs support the rebels to weaken the country."

Kasahoon nodded. "Look around you, Mr. Ambassador," he said. "We have a tremendous water supply, but our farmers depend on rain. No rain means drought. And the Egyptians, with European support, recently made an international agreement—without our consent—that Ethiopia is not allowed to use any of the Nile water for its farmers. But when the rains don't come we are allowed to starve."

NINETEEN

THE NORTHERN KINGDOM

When we arrived in Bahar-Dar it was dark. David had arranged for a hotel on the lake, a rather seedy place but quite atmospheric, with palm trees, mosquito nets over the beds, and deep old tubs.

Music drifted from the hotel's bar over the gardens, across the lawns dimly lit by colored lights. People were drinking and eating on the veranda, which looped around the main building.

"Look," said Kasahoon. "A black American family. Ethiopia was very important to black Americans through their history. I served in the southern United States when I was in the army. I saw the New Zion Church, the Abyssinian Baptist Church. For blacks, Ethiopia represented the biblical land. The black slaves in the South knew that Ethiopia was the only independent African country—and the only Christian country in Africa."

• • •

HALF A DOZEN young men hung out in the hotel's billiard room. Its walls were painted the color of dirt and a bare bulb hung from the ceiling. They went to the university in town and spoke English. They made a fuss when they learned that I was an Israeli ambassador interested in the Falashas. One took me aside and told me his name was Yacov. He was a diminutive young man, in his early twenties, just over five feet tall and very thin, dressed in blue jeans.

"I am Beta Israel," he said.

His companions scoffed.

"They think they know about me," he said. "But they don't know anything."

He pulled out his wallet. "Look," he said, shuffling through his cards. He handed me a laminated photo ID from an Israeli high-tech company based in Tel Aviv.

"My brother," he said. "A manager."

I was delighted. "You have a brother in Israel? Wonderful! When did he come?"

"It was 1981. When he was fifteen."

"And now look how nice he looks!"

Yacov was silent.

"So when do you want to make *aliyah*? I can help you."

"I don't want to come to Israel," he said.

I was shocked. "Why not?"

He just glared at me and went back to his friends.

I ASKED ZIMNA about him as we dined on the hotel terrace overlooking the lake. The tilapia, a fish native to Tana, was very fresh, caught that day.

"Maybe he's not a real Falasha," Zimna said.

"No, no. His brother must have come with Operation Moses," I said. "It's possible that you even helped him out of Sudan."

"All real Falashas want to go to Jerusalem," Zimna said.

"Not this one."

Zimna just shrugged.

"Do you want to meet him? Perhaps you can talk to him. Find out what the problem is."

Zimna put down his knife and fork and gazed out toward Tana's dark waters. A light breeze blew from the north; the lake water pulsed in small waves against the shore. Zimna was silent.

I was confused. "Do you know this brother?" And I mentioned the name of the Tel Aviv firm where he worked.

"Maybe I know about him."

"So?"

"So this is not our problem, Asher. Many Beta Israel are not happy. Maybe it can be helped and maybe not." With that he excused himself and went to bed.

WE TOOK SOME time in the morning to look around the city. It was far more pleasant than Addis, with broad palm-lined avenues, bicycle traffic, a university, provincial government offices, and a number of hotels on the lake that catered to Ethiopians on vacation.

The lake stretched from the city's northern edge. It was huge—more than fifty miles long and nearly as wide. It was dotted with islands that contained monasteries, many containing priceless illuminated manuscripts and ancient frescoes.

The Church of St. Mary of Zion in Axum was said to house the Ark of the Covenant, which no one could see but the high priests once a year. It was supposed to have been stolen by Solomon and Sheba's apocryphal son, Menelik, and brought to Ethiopia to found the new Zion when Israel became corrupt.

I suggested we go look for the Ark, but Zimna said no, that we should travel on to Gondar. He wanted to make sure we were there in good time to participate in the *Seged*. Instead, we opted to take a boat to see the Nile's source, where it debouched from the lake.

It was a short journey from the hotel dock to the narrow opening of the river. The source of the Nile! It was a peaceful scene. A fisherman on a flat boat made from reeds cast a net, water streaming off it, sparkling in the sun.

"See," I said, pointing at the thick rushes that grew on the riverbanks. "That's where he gets his boat."

"True," said Kasahoon. "But that's also where the crocodile lives. Now and then the crocodile catches the fisherman and eats him." Kasahoon laughed. "Hippos live here, too. And they can be even more dangerous than the crocodile. They are very territorial, especially the mothers when they're with their young. They're easy to kill and good to eat," he added. "Like beefsteak."

The thought made my stomach turn.

"Why not?" Kasahoon said.

"Is it kosher?"

"I don't know," David said.

"Does it chew its cud? What does it chew?"

David was thinking hard.

"What about the hoof?"

David and I were laughing. "Zimna! Do Falasha eat it?"

Zimna shrugged. His smile was polite but tepid. "Of course not. It doesn't chew its cud."

132

• • •

WE LEFT BAHAR-DAR around noon, drove around the lake's eastern shore, and came into the true north country, an area in which there were once hundreds of Falasha villages. We passed through Gondar, a small hilly city. There were beggars on the streets and the smell of sewage. People rode horses, small tough-looking beasts, bones showing through their dusty coats.

Our hotel, the Goha, was a couple of miles outside town, set high on a hill with breathtaking views of the city and the surrounding country. Its one drawback was that hot water was available only one hour in the morning, between six and seven, and at the same time in the evening. It was six when we arrived and we had to run to catch our showers.

WE WERE UP early to tour Gondar's castle compound. We knocked on big wooden doors, which were thrown open by a sleepy guard in a stained and crumpled uniform. We paid a birr. A boy slept in a shed on a pallet of straw inside the door. The guard laboriously wrote out scrawled receipts. This seemed to take half the morning. Only then were we allowed to enter.

From the inside I could see the compound was quite large, with perhaps a dozen different structures rising from grassy fields. The castles, Moorish in design, were built of the same rough brown stone as the surrounding walls.

King Fasilidas (1632–1667) had begun the castle complex when he had chosen Gondar to be the capital of the Ethiopian empire. Fasilidas had had to rebuild the country, which had been overrun by the Oromo, tribes from the south (who, today, make up 40 percent of Ethiopia's population). There has always been tension in Ethiopia between the lowland southern tribal peoples, who are largely animist and African, and the Semitic-inflected Amharit and Tigrians of the highland north.

During the era of the Oromo invasion in the sixteenth century, Ethiopia was embroiled in internal fights among regional governors. Fasilidas made Gondar the symbol of Ethiopian unity. From 1250 until Fasilidas's ascent, Ethiopia had had no fixed seat of government. The emperor, court, and army moved every few months from one province to another, living off the land and leaving only after they had exhausted all sources of food and firewood. The army numbered about fifty thousand. They fought with spears, curved swords, and shields made from elephant and buffalo hide and decorated with copper. In the sixteenth century, they had *harquebus*, introduced in battles against them by the Turks of the Ottoman Empire. Most of the men rode small sturdy horses, similar to the horses in Gondar today.

In each place they encamped, the army erected a huge tent of skins sewn together, which could accommodate hundreds of guests, petitioners, royal guards, and the royal archives with its legion of scribes. As in biblical times, all citizens had the right to demand justice from their rulers, who were obligated to sit for hours, day after day, to hear the different sides of each dispute. Most cases involved land rights and succession quarrels. The Bible was consulted—along with the Fetha-Nagast, the law of the kings. The Bible was the book used to determine the law of the land.

Magen David signs adorned some of the doors of the palace rooms, cool empty spaces floored with dark wood and white-washed walls. "We helped build these palaces," said Zimna. "And in an earlier time, in the Simian Mountains, there was a Jewish kingdom."

We were walking over rubble, ascending a dark, winding stair up a tower with slits in the stone for windows. The stairs were covered with bird droppings and the pellet-shaped dung of some small rodent, possibly rats.

"I have read about this Jewish kingdom," I said. "It lasted about three hundred years. Do you know that until Israel it was the only Jewish state in the world after the destruction of the Second Temple in Jerusalem in 70 CE? What's incredible is that it was unknown to the rest of world Jewry."

"You know of our kings Yoram and Radai?"

"Yes. And the last in the line to hold the title is Gideon, also the name of my younger son."

"I, too, Asher, have a son."

I was puzzled. "I had heard that you had a young daughter with an American wife."

"Yes, that too. But I have a first wife. A Yemenite Israeli who lives in Nathanya."

"Why did you divorce?"

He was silent a moment. "The time I was away in the refugee camps in Sudan was hard on her."

I had an uncomfortable feeling that he was blaming the Israeli government for breaking up his marriage. I didn't say anything.

Zimna excused himself and went back down the stairs. I continued up. My thoughts returned to the Jewish state. It had its ups and downs, expanding and contracting in its three hundred years of existence, from 1320 to its final defeat in 1624 at the hands of King Susenyos.

Susenyos recorded his battles against the Falashas with pride. He also recorded the heroism and tenacity of the Falasha fighters, both men and women. He demanded that the Falashas "accept Christianity or die." As he himself wrote, the Falashas did not comply; he put many of them to death because they wouldn't renounce their faith. In a bloody battle, he defeated the Falashas, killed Gideon in battle, and brought an end to the Jewish state.

Battles with Susenyos weren't the only fight the Falashas survived. King Susenyos's predecessor, King Yishak (1413–1430), also persecuted them because of their religion. Yishak wanted to unify the country under the church. He told the Falashas to convert or forfeit their right to own land.

The size of the Jewish kingdom in medieval times was estimated at one million people. Nineteenth-century travelers put the number at a quarter million. It was a primarily agricultural society, but they were also artisans. They lived in small villages. There were no big cities. Historians have said the Jewish kingdom allied itself with the Muslims against the Christians. They had an army, but they weren't completely independent. The kings were still part of the Ethiopian empire. They served under the emperor. They paid taxes to the empire. When wars occurred, it was often because they refused to pay tax.

I CAME TO the top of the turret's stair, which opened onto a small terrace. From here I could see over the walls of the castle compound and the city to the surrounding country. To the north were the impenetrable Simian Mountains, a labyrinth of jutting spires and deep canyons. This was the fastness of the Falasha kingdom.

Gondar was a strategic place because it lay at the Simians' southern edge. The city looked out over the plains to Lake Tana, which I could see glimmering in the distance. A white haze floated over the lake. The heat was building as the morning progressed. I was glad for my hat, and I shaded my eyes as I gazed toward Tana, the gateway to the south.

I looked down. Kasahoon and Zimna were below, strolling along a path through the tall grass that led to the dungeons. David was looking around anxiously. I called to him and he looked up, relieved. I picked my way down the winding stair, wiping my shoes carefully on the grass. It was time to enter the last vestiges of the kingdom.

TWENTY

AMBOVER

Our Jeeps waited for us beyond the castle gates, and we drove to Ambover, the largest Jewish village in the Gondar area and the place where Zimna had grown up. He was in a state of high excitement. Outside Gondar, the rough gravel topped a crest and a breathtaking valley appeared in front of us. We passed through fields of grain, cotton, and beans. *Tukuls* were nestled next to stone walls. There were cattle everywhere—more cows than sheep and goats.

"Asher," said Zimna, "do you know that Ethiopia has more cattle than people?"

"I can see," I said. "I do know that Ethiopia exports hides."

The road narrowed and became worse. A small creek ran along the roadside in a slit in the earth that was, perhaps, a dozen feet deep. The road followed the creek for several miles.

"I used to bathe at least once a week on Friday evenings in that creek," said Zimna. "I had to purify myself after touching a non-

Jew. And before Shabbat and holidays. Women used the water for ritual purification after menstruation. And of course, we used the creek for our drinking water and to wash our clothes!"

We came to a decrepit wooden bridge. We left the Jeeps and walked up the hill toward the village. We noticed three gentlemen approaching with two horses. Zimna looked at them as they came close, and he patted one on the back.

"Tesfaye!"

The man did a double take and then threw up his hands in delight. "Zimna!"

They embraced and rapidly kissed on alternating cheeks three times, as was customary. Then they started talking rapidly, holding each other's hands.

There were hedges to either side of the track, a dense scrub that did little to shelter us from the blazing sun. The flies swarmed, landing on our faces and hands. The smell of animal dung was strong, and I could also smell smoke.

"Soon he and his family are going to Addis," said Zimna as Tesfaye waved good-bye. "Just now he returned from Gondar where he was selling horses."

As we approached the village, Zimna became emotional. "I really couldn't return to Ambover after having tasted life in Israel," he said, speaking of leaving the village when he was fifteen for Israel. "I experienced modern life, and I was given a good education." He sighed. "I must confess. I also wanted an Israeli girl. It was hard to come back into the village where the girls knew so little of the world. Where they were so simple. I know that I was meant to return to teach in the village. But this demand was unrealistic. How could I be a new leader in this community? Against my will I returned here—to teach as planned. But there was no school, students, or budget. The government was unsympathetic to our Zionist ideas. I needed work to live. So I got a job with Solel Boneh, the Israeli construction company that built government offices in Addis. But Israel kept calling me. So when the Six Day War started, I went to buy a ticket to Israel. But by the time I landed, Israel had already won. You didn't wait for me!" He had noticed that I was listening carefully to his story, and he was grateful.

"I went to the first recruitment office I found," he continued, "to be drafted into the army. I told myself that the army would make me a complete Israeli, and that I would find other ways to help my people."

"And you did, Zimna. You're still helping!"

He nodded, but there was a sadness about him.

We came to the village, clusters of *tukuls* with no electricity or running water. Mountains rose up all around. Time had no significance in Ambover. The same way of life, of working the land, of tradition and customs, remained intact, unchanged.

We went to see the synagogue. It was a medium-sized building made of concrete, with white walls, glass windows, wooden doors back and front, and a dirt floor. The Star of David painted in the middle of the ceiling was far more moving to me than the stars on Gondar's palace doors. The synagogue's star shone on the roots of our faith. Here was Judaism as it was practiced by my ancestors in biblical times.

It was a sad sight for me. But then I realized the books strewn around were not the original Orit, the Ethiopian Torah written in Ge'ez. The books were in Hebrew, brought by the American Association for Ethiopian Jews, which had been working in Ambover for years.

Zimna said this was a new synagogue, built about on the spot where the old one existed, which had been a large *tukul*, nothing as fancy as this. He pointed out a rather large school in concrete on a hill that had been built by the Organization for Vocational Training and Skilled Trade (ORT), an Israeli agency that manages a worldwide vocational school system, mainly for Jews. Since most of the region's Falashas were already in Addis, the school was empty.

A large ledger was laid out on a table inside with signatures of foreigners from all over the world who had visited the Ambover school, beginning in 1974. The amount they had donated to the school was also recorded, as well as their comments. Few Israelis had come; the predominant nationality was American. The names were Jewish. I knew the type—I had married one. The comments showed how deeply affected the visitors had been by the sight of black Jewish children keeping the faith, thinking they were the last Jews, here at the end of the earth.

Zimna took me to see Liknesh Mahari, a fifty-eight-year-old mother with three brothers and two sisters, whom he had known as a child. She was sitting at the door of her *tukul*, wrapped in a worn *shammas* with a shawl around her head. The skin on her face was seamed, but remarkably her teeth were intact, very straight and white.

Liknesh immediately informed me that she had changed her name to Esther. "I heard the story of Esther who saved the Jews. I want to be like her." Then she lowered her gaze to the ground and said: "My father, Abarro Aimoto, died when I was five years old. My mother died seven days after his death."

I asked Esther how she lived.

"Farming," she said. "We grow bananas, coffee, wheat, barley, maize, *teff*, and cotton. We breed goats, sheep, cows, and chickens. And I want you to know that we leave 10 percent of the growth in the field for the poor to collect. They come at night, so nobody knows them. But this is not our land."

"Do you sell some of your produce?"

"We make our clothes from cotton and wool—for our own use and to sell. We are carvers and potters. We make metal tools for the farmers."

"This kind of work is considered beneath the dignity of the Ethiopian farmer," said Zimna.

I asked Esther what had happened to her husband.

"He left," she said.

"Why?"

"He found another woman."

"Younger," said Zimna.

"Falasha man?"

"Of course!" said Zimna.

"When were you married?" I asked.

"I was just a girl." Esther waved her hands in front of her face to shoo away the flies.

"How is it with divorce among Falasha?" I asked.

"The man just leaves," she said. "The husband is allowed to divorce his wife, but the wife can't divorce her husband."

"That doesn't seem fair," I said.

"That's how it is in Ethiopia," she said.

"In Israel, this will change. Right, Zimna? Didn't you tell me your wife left you?"

When Zimna translated that, she looked up at him with a sad smile.

"WE DIDN'T SEE your old house," I said to Zimna as we walked back to the Jeeps. The light was fading. Dusk came fast to this country, so close to the equator, with its twelve hours of daylight throughout the year.

Stunning Lake Tana in Ethiopia
(Picture by Camerapix, Nairobi. Courtesy of the author)

ABOVE: Hilda Naim at the
Hanukkah ceremony on the
grounds of the Israeli embassy
at what was the largest Jewish
school in the world. Addis
Ababa, Ethiopia. December
1990. *(Courtesy of the author)*

RIGHT: Zimna Berhane worked
tirelessly for the freedom of the
Beta Israel. *(Photo by Micha
Feldman. Courtesy of the author)*

Buses leaving for the airport during Operation Solomon.
Addis Ababa, Ethiopia. May 1991.
(Courtesy of the author)

Beta Israel at last in the Promised Land.
(Courtesy of the Israel Government Press Office)

The reunion of an Israeli sergeant and his immigrant mother.
(Courtesy of the Israel Government Press Office)

Kes Elihu raises the Orit—the five books of Moses—written in
the ancient Ethiopian language of Ge'ez. *(Courtesy of the author)*

A Beta Israel *kes* during a *Seged* celebration in Jerusalem.
(Courtesy of the author)

Kessim in traditional
Ethiopian dress celebrate
Seged in Jerusalem.
(Courtesy of the author)

FROM LEFT TO RIGHT: Rabbi Joseph Hadana, his mother, his father
(*Kes* of *Kes* Hadana), and the author (*Photo by Hilda Naim. Courtesy of the author*)

President George Bush and Senator Rudy Boschwitz at the White House
in 1991 reviewing Operation Solomon. (*Courtesy of Rudy Boschwitz*)

ABOVE: New friends in Jerusalem.
(Photo by Joe Malcom.
Courtesy of the author)

LEFT: Rabbi Joseph Hadana,
chief rabbi of the Ethiopian
community in Israel.
(Photo by Kenneth Wapner.
Courtesy of the author)

An Ethiopian boy at his bar mitzvah in Israel.
(Photo by Joe Malcom. Courtesy of the author)

"My house?" He shook his head. "Asher, the *tukul* is not like a house in Israel. You don't take care of it? In six months, it's gone."

"Where was it?"

He gestured vaguely up the hill.

"But what about your parents. Where did they live?"

"My parents?" Zimna was pensive. "That's another story."

I could get no more out of him.

The bridge held, just, and I found myself nodding as Kasahoon and David pushed the Jeeps hard on the way back to the hotel. Kasahoon let me rest. The darkening fields passed in a blur. The Jeep bounced along, enveloping me in a dull roar. Even with their efforts we missed the hot-water curfew. A cold shower woke me up just enough to have a quick dinner and then tumble into bed.

TWENTY-ONE

THE LAST SACRIFICE

T he next morning we arranged for our goat. David had been out walking in the early morning (right after his hot shower, which I, again, missed). Just outside Goha's grounds he had come upon the inevitable goatherd and his animals.

"Asher!" David came running. "Come. Let's take one. They look very nice."

We brought Kasahoon in to negotiate, and soon we had a small goat for which we paid 120 birr, only a 20 percent *faranji* surcharge. "He can keep the skin!" I had said to Kasahoon. "It's a very small goat, no more than a kid," said David. Finally, we wore the poor man down. After we had cinched the deal, I slipped him twenty birr. I really just wanted to bargain.

The hotel kitchen was initially reluctant to take on the task of cooking the goat, but when I told them the four of us would take only a quarter and distribute the rest among the staff, everyone got into the swing of things. The goat would be grilled outside that evening.

I SPENT THE day in Gondar, on the hotel phone to the embassy, and catching up on paperwork. At about four I came to see how the kitchen was doing. They were valiantly cutting the meat into small pieces with crude iron knives. They seasoned it with spices and salt, and rubbed oil into it. Then they set a fire out in the courtyard. Roses bloomed around our table, with its splendid view of Gondar and Tana in the distance.

Boys came, their arms full of sticks. A fire was made on a stone patio. When it had burned down, out came the chef, wearing a white jacket and hat and carrying a platter of goat meat. He cooked it on a flat thin pan on the fire. It looked and smelled delicious, and it was tasty, but very tough.

"This goat is tough from running up and down the hills," I said.

"I wish he had spent more time sleeping," said David.

"Ethiopian goats are very strong," said Kasahoon, his white teeth flashing.

A huge pile of the meat was set before us on the table, and we gnawed, our jaws working hard, trying not to break our teeth.

Zimna would not touch it.

"Give it a try, Zimna," I kept urging him through the meal.

When we finished it was dark.

"Why wouldn't you eat the goat? I got it specially for you."

Zimna shrugged. "I didn't want to say it in front of David. But it's not kosher."

"Oh, Zimna, I'm sorry. I told them to make the knife sharp," I lied.

"That's all right. Tomorrow is the *Seged*, and I want to be especially careful."

ZIMNA WAS IN an emotional state, looking at the mountain north of Ambover, where the *Seged* was celebrated each year on the twenty-ninth day of the eighth month of Heshvan, in accordance with the lunar calendar.

Seged means "to bow." Scholars are unclear how the holiday developed. It marked the moment when Moses received the Ten Commandments on Sinai and commemorated Ezra's call on the Israelites to observe the Torah and not to lose their identity through intermarriage. Beta Israel would walk from all over the region, sometimes for days, to attend the *Seged*. That was also the custom in ancient times when the Israelites would visit Jerusalem three times a year to make sacrifice in the Temple.

It was a clear cool morning, the fields of *teff* and barley glowing and green. We crossed the river that ran out of the Gondar and the Simians through the Ambover valley into Tana. Zimna was somber. He seemed to be nostalgic in spite of himself. I sensed these were not feelings he wanted to revisit, as though the archaic Judaism with which he had grown up was wrestling inside him with the mantle of rabbinic Judaism he had taken on in Israel.

As we approached the mountain, Zimna said, "This whole area surrounding Ambover is naturally protected from outside intruders, either troublemakers or those who seek to steal animals or *teff*." He pointed to the mountaintops. "On top of these mountains, at certain times, or when there was trouble brewing, we installed Beta Israel guards who served as a deterrent against intruders, particularly during festivities like the *Seged* when so many people with women and children are on the move, bringing a goat or a sheep for sacrifice."

We were able to drive almost to the foot of the mountain. The last of the dew was burning off the grass. There were, perhaps, a couple of hundred people, men and women, young and old. "This may be the last *Seged* in Ethiopia," Zimna said. "When I was a child, thousands gathered."

I saw a *kes* at the head of the crowd, carrying the Orit wrapped in sacred cloth on top of his head. He was dressed in a white robe with a brightly colored red-and-green shawl. He carried a colorful umbrella and wore a white turban on his head. Elders gathered around him. They, too, carried sacred books.

Many of the younger men carried stones. "They carry them to harden their climb, as a symbol of devotion to God," said Zimna. "Also, the stones will serve to build a circle around the *kes* when he leads the ceremony on the mountaintop."

The morning was still cool, the sun low. The air was powdered with a fine dust. I looked up. The mountain seemed very high above us, a craggy skull of jutting rocks and yellow earth, stunted trees clinging to its side.

"Zimna! We're going all the way to the top?"

He nodded. "The climb may take two hours. The ceremony is hours more. Then we walk back. For all this time, we fast."

Already my stomach was grumbling and my mouth felt dry.

"Now you're going to be a real Beta Israel, Asher."

THE *KES* STARTED climbing slowly upward, quoting from memory passages from the Orit and other scriptures. He was followed by the elders, the stone carriers, and the rest of the congregation.

At the beginning, the climb was a breeze. I had strength from my good night's rest and the fresh morning air. The path rose out of the valley and I could see Gondar in the distance. But soon the sun was on top of us, getting stronger by the minute. Sweat trickled into my eyes. My shirt stuck to my back.

A keening rose from the stones and grass, small insects buzzing in the rising heat. Zimna walked next to me, eyes on the ground, his lips moving silently. The women bowed down, putting cupped hands in front of their faces and moving them in a circular imprecation. Men beat on two-headed kettledrums (called *nagarit*) with curved wooden sticks. They blew small brass horns that had a cadence somewhere between Armenia and Tibet, and they rang small handheld gongs. People erupted in prayer. They prostrated themselves on the path. They lifted their eyes to the heavens and raised their hands in supplication.

I was transported back to the time when the Children of Israel ascended Mount Zion to the Temple in the Jerusalem, where worship took place in the open air, in a high place, close to nature.

I suddenly felt fatigued. The congregation began to pass me by, moving inexorably upward at a steady tempo. They didn't seem to be affected by the climb or the sun. Zimna tried to console me. "In Ethiopia we walk a lot. It's part of our lives."

On top of the mountain, there was a flat area of packed dirt with a spectacular view north to Gondar and south to Tana. The wind blew over the grassy summit. Sweat cooled on my body. The stone carriers rushed to create the circle for the *kes*.

Everyone gathered around as he read from the Orit, reciting the Ten Commandments. The congregation, mostly illiterate, didn't understand the ancient language, but they expressed their submission to God by constant bowing. The bows went lower and lower until foreheads touched the stony ground. They sang, too—songs that reminded me of the Arabic- and Persian-inflected Yemenite liturgy. They covered their eyes with their hands. Women ululated, rolling their eyes up until only the whites showed, vibrating their shoulders and breasts. Whenever the *kes* made a blessing in Amharic, the congregants responded with vigor, their excitement grew, and the drums and horns were drowned out by the congregants' voices.

The *kes* read from the book of Nehemiah, who, in the sixth century BCE, led the returnees from the Babylonian exile back to Jerusalem. He found that the Israelites who hadn't been in exile but had stayed in Jerusalem had intermarried with gentile women and failed to keep the Torah's commandments.

I began to feel faint from the sun and the climb. I wanted to sit down, but there was nowhere to sit and no one was sitting. We sang and prayed, and finally, with a great clamor and cries up to heaven, the ceremony ended. The Beta Israel danced down the mountain. They freely sang. Finally, we were back in Ambover, where everyone gathered near the synagogue.

Adjacent to the synagogue was an enclosure where Zimna said the *kes* would sacrifice an ox.

"Can we watch?" I asked.

Zimna thought a moment. "Yes. I think so. We are not lepers. We have no open wounds, and we don't have black skin."

"What is this black skin?"

"It means you come from an adulterous birth."

I was intrigued. "Who else is not allowed in?"

"Falashmura," he said—Jews who had converted to Christianity in the last hundred years. "Girls raped and not pardoned by their parents. Men bitten by a hyena, and anyone who has sex on Shabbat."

THE BEAST WAS brought from nearby, people dancing and singing around it. It was led onto a low rectangular stone altar and roped around the legs. Three people held it tight. The ox flailed and kicked, its hooves all over, breath steaming out its snout.

The *kes* approached and took a special knife from a table nearby. He checked it to make sure the blade was clean and sharp. As he approached, the ox's head was forced to the side, revealing its throat. With a swift motion, the *kes* cut and blood spilled out. The ox gave a fierce movement with its feet, shaking, trembling, its breath coming quick and then quickly subsiding. Blood pooled on the ground; the ox seemed to sigh, sag, and then suddenly its legs buckled beneath it and its eyes dimmed.

All this time the Beta Israel prayed. They never stopped. Two people dragged the ox from the altar to the ground and cut away different parts of the skin. Then they hacked the meat into pieces, which were brought to the fire. As prescribed in the Torah, certain portions of the sacrifice were given to God.

BEING MY USUAL squeamish self, I didn't eat the ox, but Zimna relished it. Fortunately, we had brought some fruit and bread in the Jeep, and I broke my fast with that.

The image of the legs buckling under the beast haunted me long after we had left.

"Zimna," I said as we were driving back to the hotel at dusk, "do you miss this kind of Judaism?"

He sighed. "No. It is finished."

He was right. We had seen the last sacrifice here in the mountains of Ethiopia. But I wasn't sad. There was no room anymore for this kind of practice. Sacrifice was a way to appease God; it was about wish-fulfilling prayers, fear and superstition. After the practice of sacrifice ceased, the religion had become incorporeal, which, I think, is one of its great strengths.

That the Falashas kept to the faith without the Mishnah and Talmud is doubly extraordinary. The Talmud was compiled by rabbis in the sixth century CE from the vast oral interpretations and exegesis that had developed over the centuries around the Torah, Mishnah, and, to a lesser degree, the prophetic books of the Old Testament.

The Talmud is the basis of rabbinic Judaism—a living text that grew through the Middle Ages as the rabbis spun webs of interpretation around interpretation, labyrinthine systems through which they traveled in a lifetime of devotion. Talmudic study cross-pollinated among the Diaspora communities of Europe, North Africa, and Asia Minor, producing a highly evolved and richly nuanced body of faith, morality, philosophy, theology, and law.

The Beta Israel had been left behind. In the buckling legs and dimming eyes I had witnessed something that I had read about in the Bible but had never imagined that I'd see. It was an honor to be there, to experience it, and then to put it to rest.

TWENTY-TWO

MINION

Back in Addis, I prepared for the arrival of Hilda and Ronit, my daughter. Adanich scrubbed every corner of the suite. For the first time she cleaned the two verandas and insisted that the hotel paint the rooms. She also pushed me to ask the manager of the hotel to change the living room furniture and put in a new dining room set.

On the day of their arrival a basket of flowers and a basket of fruit were delivered to my door, compliments of the Hilton's manager. I wondered how the women in my life would like their new environment. Ronit had taken a two-week vacation from her work as an aide for cultural affairs to the Israeli consul general in Los Angeles, and Hilda had been teaching English in Jerusalem.

When Hilda and Ronit stepped off the plane I asked them for their first impression. "The people are so pleasant," Hilda said. Ronit agreed. That is often the reaction of people coming into contact with Ethiopians. Our car was allowed right up to the exit door, so the women were spared the polio beggars who haunt the airport's precincts, propelling themselves on their arms, their legs twisted stumps. Hilda had served with me in Kenya. She had seen polio beggars; she had been beset by hordes of flies. But the poverty and disease in Ethiopia was far deeper than in Kenya; I didn't want her put off first thing.

Hilda and I sank into the Peugeot's backseat; Ronit slid in up front with Konata. I could sense my daughter drinking in the scenery, excited and sparkling even after her long journey. On the way to the hotel, she reported on the doings of her brothers, who were both students at Drexel University in Philadelphia. It made me happy that they were in constant touch.

Hilda gave me news on tensions in the Gulf—the threat of war if Saddam Hussein failed to retreat from Kuwait.

"There is deep concern in Israel," she said. "We know that he's a wild person. Unpredictable."

"Yes," I said. "Attacking Israel is the best way he has to break the Arab alliance with the United States."

"People are cleaning out their bomb shelters. I cleaned ours," she said in a pointed way.

Ronit glanced over her shoulder.

"*Oy vay!*" I said, remembering all the papers, broken furniture, and other odds and ends that I had stored down there, feeling guilty that Hilda had to deal with that mess. It's the law in Israel: Every house or apartment has to have a shelter; in peacetime, we put them to other uses. But then Hilda smiled indulgently at me. I could tell she had missed me, and I was flooded with a sense of relief. Here, finally, was my closest friend. The person I could talk to most freely, in a completely unguarded way. The feeling of isolation that had enshrouded me since I had landed in Addis five weeks ago suddenly lifted like a fog. I felt bright and warm.

I pointed out landmarks as we made our way through the Bole

neighborhood in the southeastern part of the city, winding upward through the streets, gaining elevation.

The suite made a good impression on both of them, as did Adanich. Ronit was her usual voluble self—a typical Israeli girl with a comment and opinion about everything. She insisted on assisting Adanich with lunch. I watched my daughter as she moved about—strong, energetic, and sincere. She didn't need to be told what to do; she made her own way. With all the privilege of the diplomatic world in which she had grown up, there was nothing spoiled about her.

I suggested after lunch that the women swim and rest, but they refused to linger. They had come to work, not loaf, and they wanted to get to the embassy as soon as possible and begin helping with the processing of applications, or in the clinic, or school. We weren't sure where they would best fit in.

It took them precisely one hour to find their niche. By midafternoon, Hilda was teaching Hebrew in a *tukul* and Ronit, the artist-painter-photographer-ceramist, had organized twenty girls into a class on ceramics.

We settled into a comfortable routine, traveling together to the embassy. They left me to my own devices, and I didn't interfere with them. In the evening, Konata collected us and we returned to the Hilton together.

HILDA HAS PLAYED a very important role in diplomatic work, and her contribution in Addis soon began to be felt. The hotel suite was transformed into a home, a place where we entertained. Hilda quickly established close relations with the wives of high brass in the military, government, and business communities. Soon they were coming to the Hilton to dine. With Adanich and Ronit, before she returned to LA, Hilda prepared wonderful dinners. I learned the mood of the country, got inside gossip on the government, and forged connections with the country's elite, which I could draw on during the day when I needed information or help.

Hilda also helped me cultivate relationships with eight Yemenite Jewish families who lived in Addis, all merchants, remnants of a former large and prosperous Jewish community of several hundred. There was a synagogue in the private compound of Shlomo Shalamey, a pale man of seventy with sparse hair, watery blue eyes, and an irrepressible sense of humor, who was considered the head of the Yemenis. He served as a *shochet* (kosher slaughterer), conducted Sabbath services, and was a good source of food in a city where food was hard to get.

The Yemenite Jewish community in Ethiopia was extremely prosperous. Shlomo owned several square blocks of residential buildings and shops. He had managed to retain many of his holdings, even during Mengistu's regime. The flow of goods in and out of the country through his holding companies abated but had far from ceased. He still made money, along with the rest of the community. It is a particular Jewish talent—to stay afloat during the turbulence of internal political struggles and upheavals.

There had been setbacks, of course, about which Shalamey and others moaned and groaned. Real estate had been seized. Textile interests had been nationalized, or seminationalized—it was hard to fathom their secretive dealings. Shalamey prevailed upon me to help him with the banks. The community had come across the Red Sea from Aden, which had been a Crown colony until 1968 when the British had withdrawn and Aden had been absorbed by Yemen. They held British passports, but the British did not consider them subjects. They were too international, submerged in their nomadic skein of commercial contacts. Their children lived in Israel; their wives in England or Canada. The men spent most of their time in Addis, wheeling and dealing, looking after their interests, growing richer, rising to lofty heights above the indigence that surrounded them. They were careful, however, to maintain a low profile; they were discreet.

They put themselves, at least in part, above the Falashas. There was a telling incident. One Saturday morning, for Shabbat service, they needed a *minion,* the ten Jewish men (according to the Orthodox view) required in order to perform certain prayers and remove the Torah scroll from the Ark in the synagogue. Should the Falashas be counted in a *minion?* Some Yemenites said yes (Shlomo among them). Others said no. Four Falasha men were in attendance at the synagogue, which was tucked away upstairs behind the iron gate and high walls of one of Shlomo's warehouses and offices. Much to my chagrin, the Yemenites refused to count them, leaving us short of a *minion* by two.

"What is this?" I asked Shlomo, looking around in distress. The shabby room was bare but for battered chairs, the Ark, and a large black-framed photo of a bearded rabbi, the bottomless wells of his eyes filled with sadness and compassion. The atmosphere reeked of an insidious excuse for piety. I wondered what the *hacham* rabbi on the wall would have made of the current scene. Would he have sagely nodded his approval?

Shlomo simply shrugged off my question. The Falasha men did not seem to know what was going on. There was a quick huddle. Two of the Yemenites broke off and hustled downstairs to call the embassy for the required two. It was ridiculous. Most of the embassy personnel were lackadaisically observant; they did not go to synagogue in Israel. Abroad they went out of homesickness or guilt, or when they could be persuaded: It added glamour to the local Jewish community to have diplomatic guests. And here were the Falashas who had been sticklers, adhering scrupulously to the letter of law as laid down in the Torah, as their ancestors had before them.

Two young men from the embassy eventually appeared, sleepy-eyed, unshaven—and only then could we begin.

"Yitgadel veit kadash shmey rabba."

We chanted Kaddish.

TWENTY-THREE

HORSEHAIR

Hilda was excited about the close relationship she was developing with some of the Beta Israel women. Her encounters with them gave her a privileged glimpse into a fascinating, exotic world. But one Sunday morning, on our way to the Mercato, I noticed she was tight and silent.

"What's wrong?" I asked.

She turned to face me, her face filled with pain. "It's terrible. What I heard today from the women."

"Why are you whispering?"

"I don't want Konata to hear."

"Why?"

"Because I'm embarrassed! Enough now, Asher."

As we approached the Mercato, the streets narrowed. Traffic slowed. We crawled through an arcade of Muslim rug and fabric shops. The men wore tarbooshes and white or blue jabootis. They ritualistically washed their hands from spigots, which sprouted from their stoops, unrolling mats and bowing north and east toward Mecca in midday prayer.

In the Mercato, we were immediately besieged by the car-park boys, who staked out space on the curbs and held it against all comers. They jumped around, clearing a path through the throngs. It wasn't such a bad deal. A few birr bought you a space and protection from the hooves of beasts, the wobbling carts, the swaggering trucks.

Konata, of course, did not consort with these types. He shooed them away from the Peugeot, lording over it, arms folded across his chest. He was a man of consequence in his suit, leaning against the gleaming sedan, oblivious to their petty bounding.

Hilda and I picked our way across the gutter to the curb. The din of the market enveloped us. Its smell of excrement and rot caused us to fold into ourselves, breathe lightly, take care what we touched and where we stepped.

"What a stench," said Hilda.

"Please, madam, take care," said Konata, eyeing askance the car-park boys. "There are many thieves here."

The minute we were out of his hearing, Hilda turned to me. "I learned something horrible today. Girls may marry at the age of twelve. The boy is usually a little older, but sometimes they marry men old enough to be their father!"

"So. This we already knew. It's not so terrible!"

"Give me a minute, Asher!"

"Today I met Yehudit," she went on, "who said she knew you."

"I was impressed with her, and with Rivka, since my first day at the embassy."

"She's an exceptional person! She speaks her mind, perhaps because she's suffered so much. She wanted to learn Hebrew, but at the age of twenty-three she was embarrassed to go to the *tukul* with the kids. So I've been giving her private lessons. She knows some English and today she opened up to me."

Here Hilda stopped and went over to investigate some lovely-looking plum tomatoes.

"What did she say?"

"I'm coming to it." Hilda walked over to a vegetable stand and weighed a plum tomato in her palm. "When she was fourteen," Hilda continued, "her father arranged for her to marry Girma, a widower of fifty-two, the father of four boys. Girma was already gray-haired. Three of his children were older than she was. How could she fulfill the role of mother? But the *shiduch* wasn't so bad. Even though he was a Jew, Girma had a good job in the government. He had a house and savings."

I noticed that the vendor was charging much more than the regular price for the vegetables that Hilda chose. Although I knew that Hilda would not take kindly to the interruption, I could not resist embroiling myself in a protracted negotiation. Tomatoes, Falashas—I can't resist a good fight.

Hilda finally interceded. "Asher, enough already. What's the difference? Ten cents. Let's go!" I grudgingly handed over a limp and tattered bill. The bills in Ethiopia looked like they had been sucked on for nourishment and then stomped on in the gutter. They were unsavory, to say the least. Hilda wouldn't handle them.

Hilda took my arm. "Two years after her wedding," she said, "Yehudit gave birth to twin boys. Eighteen months later both died from typhus. Yehudit almost had a nervous breakdown. She was partially consoled three years later when she became pregnant again. Girma insisted that she consult a fortune-teller, who said she was bearing a girl. Girma demanded that she abort. He wanted a boy. Yehudit refused. 'You already have four boys,' she told him. Never tender, Girma now subjected her to constant insults and frequent beatings. His family, too, joined in, pressuring her to obey her husband. But Yehudit refused. Meanwhile, Girma acquired another lover. Yehudit decided she had had enough and escaped to Addis on her own."

"You know, it's extraordinary for an Ethiopian woman to run away like that. Unheard of!"

"I know," said Hilda.

We had slowed. Absorbed by what she was saying I had failed to note the number of people who surrounded us, all pushing to sell us merchandise—cigarettes, matches, small ceramic sculptures, and combs—or simply begging for alms. I distributed ten-cent coins and with fast steps we moved on, entering a section of the market that sold gold jewelry. Necklaces and bracelets were draped, gleaming, in ostentatious displays in the shop windows. The jewelry was of uniformly uninspired workmanship. Shop after shop had the same items, the same designs. The pieces were sold not by their craft but by the gram. Relatively well-heeled women in clean *shammas* fingered the wares.

The sun blazed overhead. People were thick around us, the smells overpowering. I loved the teeming life of it, its humanity and color, but I understood when Hilda said, "I've had enough."

"Okay, let's go."

KONATA HAD BEEN watching us, and when he saw us turn, looking for the car, he quickly stepped out, approaching us and taking our bags. It was with relief that we settled into the car's quiet interior.

"Sir?"

"Ice cream," I replied, eager to placate my wife.

The car inched out of the market and soon we cruised along the decrepit boulevards.

The American ice-cream parlor was close to the Mercato. Its customers were mainly foreign with a few well-to-do Ethiopians. I ordered my usual—pistachio and chocolate; Hilda had chocolate and vanilla. The dish was served with a biscuit and mineral water.

I had thought we were through with Yehudit, but that was not the case.

"Yehudit," said Hilda, "says that girls are married young for their protection; Ethiopians won't violate a married woman."

"But how can a marriage be consummated at such an early age?"

"You don't understand. There is a sequence. First the bride has to prove her virginity. She sits on a low chair and three old women peer at her from underneath. If they declare that she's 'clean like the water' that means that her virginity is intact. After the wedding ceremony, the bride moves to the bridegroom's house. But she stays with the parents in their hut until they deem that she is 'physically mature.' Only then do the parents build a separate *tukul* for the new couple, who are then allowed to 'unite' under one roof."

All this Hilda said with no small degree of sarcasm.

"What happens," I asked, "if the bride doesn't like her parents' choice?"

"Normally, her parents don't force her to marry against her will."

Two young men, sitting close to us, were trying to follow Hilda's talk. So we moved to another corner of the parlor. Hilda sat close to me and lowered her voice: "Asher, have you heard of clitorectomy?"

"Yes, it's prevalent throughout sub-Saharan Africa."

Hilda paused. My wife is a strong woman, not easily given to tears, but now I saw them gathering in her eyes.

"You mean the Falasha, too, perform clitorectomy?"

She nodded, speechless.

"Hilda," I said. "You and I know that the Bible says nothing about clitorectomy. It is not a religious command, and maybe even contradicts Jewish tradition. But the Falashas' treatment of women is a weird blend of Judaic law and African tribal practices."

"When they come to Israel, this practice will not last one day," she said. "Yehudit says Falashas practice clitorectomy when and where their neighbors practice it."

"Why do they do this?" I asked.

"They think by depriving a woman of sexual pleasure she will not be tempted to be unfaithful. She will be less demanding, and learn to fulfill only the man's desires. But I think it is more than that, Asher. They mean to make her subservient. Limit her freedom. Deprive her of her individuality. Sex is the one area where woman have some power over men. Men fear a woman's sexuality. Clitorectomy deprives her of even this!" She banged her fist against the table, and I reared back in my chair. Her words felt like blows. "What is more, the procedure is done in an unsanitary environment and results in crushing pains."

I took a breath. "Did Yehudit tell you how and when it's done?"

"Older women do it. They use a knife. Mostly they make a cut in the clitoris and let it bleed. Other tribes, particularly the Muslims, remove the clitoris altogether and sew up the clitoris and vulva with horsehair to prevent the girl from having sex until the stitches are opened by the husband." The image was so

163

graphic I turned pale. "It is performed when the girl is nine days old. The woman never enjoys sex, lives in constant pain, and suffers horribly every time she gives birth."

BACK AT THE HILTON that evening I had a massage with Yusef, a blind man, well into his sixties, who had worked as the emperor's masseur. Yusef worked oil into my back and shoulders. I couldn't stop thinking about what Hilda had told me. Was this one of the ways the Muslim man enforced polygamy? It was hard enough to satisfy just one woman, one wife, let alone three or four. The squelching of sexual desire was a way to keep a woman from seeking other men.

"How does that feel, sir?" Yusef asked.

"Fine," I said. But, in truth, I was oddly numb. I couldn't feel a thing.

CORNERED

While I had been touring in the north and getting Hilda settled, Kasa had flown to Washington. He went to the Congress. He met Senator Alan Cranston of California. Everywhere he tried to portray Mengistu as ready to change his policies. But his words fell on deaf ears.

Secretary of State James Baker received Kasa in New York. As Kasa explained the reasons for delay in mass emigration of Beta Israel, blaming mistakes on Israeli application forms, Baker (who likes to tell it as it is) interrupted him. "You just let them go," he said curtly, ending the meeting.

When he met Lubrani in Washington in the meeting I had arranged, Kasa asked for a hundred-million-dollar loan. It was pure blackmail. "He hopes to buy tanks at a bargain-basement rate in Cuba with the money," said Houdek when he heard. Lubrani told Kasa, in polite terms, to go fly a kite.

• • •

His U.S. mission a failure, Kasa switched the battleground to Israel. In the first week of December, he landed in Tel Aviv, hoping to extract money or arms from us. In retrospect, I think he knew that this was his last hurrah. He was the one who had advocated using the Falashas to pressure Israel to help Mengistu. If he failed to get results, what use was he?

Divon met him at the airport and put him up in a hotel on the beach in Tel Aviv.

Kasa didn't indicate for how long he was going to stay. He was our guest, but a guest who invited himself on our account—and what a big account it turned out to be!

Kasa felt at home in Israel. He had friends from the time when he had been a student in Jerusalem. Many of them had become decision makers. Also, he knew most of the former Israeli ambassadors who had served in Ethiopia, and who had visited his father, a minister in Haile-Selassie's cabinet. Lately, Kasa had made acquaintances in the Israeli intelligence community during his service as Ethiopian ambassador in Geneva (which is a watering trough for spies).

From day one, he was busy contacting old and new acquaintances from all branches of government, as well as businesspeople, trying to amass advocates to extend help to "embattled Ethiopia."

I flew to Israel on business, not connected to Kasa's trip. On landing at Ben-Gurion airport, I called Divon for an update.

"Two weeks have passed and we still don't know when this visit ends."

"Where is he staying?"

"On the beach, at the Tel Aviv Hilton. He is enjoying himself, but he is getting nowhere reversing Israel's refusal to get involved in Ethiopia's civil war."

"Does he really believe he can succeed?"

"I don't know. But he is a very persuasive person and an excellent advocate. I would hire him as my lawyer anytime. I have arranged for you to meet Rafi (I omit his surname; he is from intelligence) who has been tailing Kasa at the Atara coffee shop on Allemby Street at 10:30 A.M. I knew you would want to find out immediately what he's been doing."

TEL AVIV IS only a thirty-minute drive from the airport. I felt the deep joy that I always feel upon returning to Israel. I traveled on the four lanes of the Ayalon Highway to the sea.

I had time before my meeting with Rafi, so I checked out the Hilton. It was very posh, right on the beach, with two swimming pools. Many elegant ladies paraded through the lobby—I knew Kasa would like that. The large restaurant on the first floor served food around the clock. Next to the restaurant was the bar.

With all these conveniences, who would want to return to the gloomy situation in Addis? Suddenly, I had an embarrassing thought: What would happen if Kasa saw me? How would I explain my presence? I turned around and took Allemby Street to the Atara.

Rafi was waiting for me. I had met him once before in Jerusalem. He was in his late twenties, blond, with a cool demeanor. He talked softly and slowly, one eye on the passing scene. He was relaxed but alert.

"The guy is very active," Rafi began. "He is seeing many people and some very important ones."

I ordered a coffee. "What does he say to the people he meets?"

"Many things. Some of them may be convincing in other circumstances. He says that if the rebels take over, Ethiopia will turn Muslim and become our enemy. He argues that it is in our interest to support Mengistu's Christian regime."

I whistled. "You can't underestimate this man."

"That's not all. He says the Arab countries have taken revenge for Ethiopia's renewal of diplomatic relations with Israel by supplying arms to the rebels. 'The rebels receive arms from the Arabs and yet Israel denies us aid?' He bullies, threatens, and cajoles. He makes people feel guilty. 'Mengistu is not interested in the ten-million-dollar aid package in health and agriculture!' " said Rafi, doing a good imitation of Kasa. " 'We need help to defend ourselves. If we don't get it, you will be judged by history!' He's very dramatic!"

"What about the Beta Israel? Does he mention them?"

"Only to say that emigration is proceeding too slowly and that inefficiency in your embassy is what's holding it up."

"*Oy vay.*"

"He lies beautifully," said Rafi with genuine admiration in his voice.

I WENT TO Jerusalem for meetings at the Foreign Ministry. The consensus was there was not much we could do that we weren't doing already to speed Falasha emigration. Four days later, I took Alitalia to Rome to connect with Ethiopia Airlines to Addis. Before my departure, Divon told me that Kasa showed no signs of leaving.

Divon said that Kasa's bills kept mounting, especially his bar bill. Was he drinking too much? We were concerned that Kasa was afraid to return and face Mengistu without money or arms.

Was impending doom impelling him to live it up—on our tab? Worse, we speculated, he might ask Israel for asylum. That would be a political disaster vis-à-vis Mengistu, whose favor we were seeking.

SEVERAL DAYS AFTER I was back in Addis, I received a call from Divon.

"Our guest left this morning to the relief of us all!" he said. I was relieved that I wouldn't have to deal with asylum. But it meant that the battleground had shifted again to my domain—Addis.

Kasa called me at ten that night when I was preparing for bed in my suite.

"Asher, I asked your people to address my two suitcases directly to Addis via Cairo," he roared. "The suitcases didn't arrive with me. Are they being held because your people are not finished reading my secret documents?"

He did not catch me off-guard. I knew how Kasa would react to the failure of his travels—like a cornered animal. I promised to look into the matter immediately. The following morning I was happy to tell him that his two suitcases had, indeed, arrived in Cairo with El Al, but Cairo had failed to put them on the Ethiopian plane.

He didn't say anything. He had wanted something to hold over me. In that moment, I almost felt sorry for him.

TWENTY-FIVE

SCUDS OVER TEL AVIV

Let me not be sheltered from dangers, but to be
fearless in facing them.

—*Rabindranath Tagore*

S oon after, on January 16, the United States bombed
Baghdad. On the eighteenth, Saddam Hussein fired Scud
missiles at Tel Aviv. Lubrani was in a bunker when I
reached him by phone. We had to carefully assess the situation.
When tensions in the Gulf had escalated, Hilda and Ronit had
returned to Israel. I, of course, wanted to be with them. And I also
wanted to be in Israel when she was under attack, to lend whatever help I could; but I felt that I was needed in Addis to continue
negotiations.

ON JANUARY 23 at 8:00 A.M., while I was having breakfast, I
received a call from a Mr. Tadesse, assistant to the chief of protocol: "Mr. Ambassador, the president wishes to see you at 8:30 A.M."

"You mean this morning?" I mumbled. "Now?"

"Yes, sir. Sorry for the rush."

"Can you please tell me the subject of the meeting so I can pre-pare?"

"No, sir."

Adanich was surprised to see me abruptly leave my breakfast and put on my jacket and tie. She ran to the veranda to warn Konata. I was nervous. Presidents don't call ambassadors in this way. Was Mengistu cutting diplomatic relations with Israel and sending me packing?

I don't know if I feared the worst—or hoped for it. I wasn't concerned for my safety. I didn't believe that even a homicidal brute like Mengistu would touch me, no matter how much favor he might think he would be able to curry from the so-called moderate Arab states for making my life miserable or end-ing it.

But if he expelled me, what would happen to the Beta Israel? I hated to think, and was surprised when I realized that my alle-giance—the deep commitment I have to both family and country (and for an Israeli of my generation, these two groups are blurred)—had shifted subtly over the past ten weeks to include the lost tribe.

AT MENGISTU'S PALACE, Mrs. Sheune was waiting for me. She led me straight into the president's office. She seemed partic-ularly dour and fearsome. But my worry changed when I saw Mengistu's smiling face. He beckoned me to sit next to him.

"I have great admiration for the leaders of Israel," he said. "They are nation builders and defend the security of the country with great courage."

"Thank you, Mr. President," I said. "For your kind words."

"I called you to express my deep sorrow for the casualties Iraqi missiles have caused Israel. Israel has acted with restraint, but I would like you to tell your government that Israel has the right to defend herself."

"Thank you for your valuable support. I will send your words of sympathy to the Israeli families who were affected by the attacks. The U.S. government has asked us not to retaliate. Israel's military response would play into Saddam Hussein's hands, breaking the Arab coalition against Hussein built by America."

THE WHOLE MEETING lasted less than fifteen minutes. I returned to the Hilton. An Ethiopian television team was waiting in my suite to interview me on the Gulf crisis. They gave me twenty minutes live. That was the first and last television interview I had in Addis. Later, I leaned that Mengistu had held similar meetings with the U.S., British, Saudi Arabian, and Egyptian ambassadors.

From the interview, I went to the embassy. There were people milling about outside the *masged* and voices from within. I entered. It was full of men, most of them sitting on the ground, talking. *Kes* Hadana was standing, leaning on his staff. He beckoned to me, said a word to one of the men around him, briefly disappeared, and then returned with a packet of letters.

"*Exaver immasgen Israel*"—God bless Israel.

I had no idea what these letters were. I went immediately up to my office and opened them. They were from the Beta Israel, expressing support for Israel "in its difficult time" and condemning Saddam. They were spontaneous letters, some written in Amharic, others in English, with big letters and mistakes.

Most were not signed. In dictatorial regimes, citizens don't interfere in the affairs of state. The letters could have put the writers in danger. Even though Mengistu expressed support for Israel, he was notoriously two-faced. I sent the letters in a sealed diplomatic pouch to the Foreign Ministry in Jerusalem. I didn't want Mengistu's thugs to get their hands on them, and I wanted the ministry to see this testimony of the Beta Israel's loyalty.

TWENTY-SIX

A THOUSAND AND ONE NIGHTS

T o soften the return of Kasa empty-handed from his trip, Lubrani arranged for the visit of two Jewish business magnates from England: Sir David Alliance from Liverpool, one of the largest textile producers in Europe, and Sami Shimeon, Europe's largest vegetable and fruit marketer. Hearing that these two economic giants were going to visit a place like Addis in the middle of a civil war had a tremendous influence on the Ethiopian government. Even Kasa was impressed.

Lubrani flew in for the visit. We met the two Londoners in the VIP room of the Addis airport. David, in his early fifties, was small and dapper, with dark hair. He wore an expensive, elegant gray lightweight suit with white shirt and checkered blue tie. Sami was a bit older, in his late fifties, heavyset, more disheveled than David, his suit rumpled. Both spoke Hebrew. Most Sephardic Jews learn to read the Bible in the original in Hebrew. Growing up in Tripoli, my experience was similar to theirs. I attended Talmud Torah, a Jewish school, every afternoon after spending the morning in the *scuola elementare*, an Italian school.

We welcomed our guests and blessed them in Hebrew for the important mission they had taken upon themselves—a mission to liberate Jews from bondage.

"*Zu mitzvah!*" they answered—it is a good deed.

"We are also serious about doing business here," David added. "If what they have to offer makes sense."

Sami chimed in, "The Beta Israel issue is what motivated us to come. But our ears are open."

DAVID VISITED ETHIOPIA'S old and inefficient textile factories. He made a generous proposal, promising to completely modernize the plants, train workers and management, and then buy what the plants produced. But he made it clear that this offer was contingent on the government allowing Ethiopian Jews to emigrate to Israel. Sami made a similar proposal, developing farms in the Awash region to export produce to Saudi Arabia.

These two propositions would have been extraordinary even in normal times, let alone during a civil war. No one in his right mind would have invested in Ethiopia. Was this an exhibition of Jewish solidarity? Or empty promises that these businessmen knew they wouldn't have to keep? The government was busy with survival, focused on only one thing—trying to live through the next rebel attack. They couldn't possibly work out a long-term economic plan.

THE LAST NIGHT the Brits were in town, Kasa threw a dinner party. He sent two Mercedes at seven, which drove us to Bole. As usual, I was talking, so I didn't notice our route. Suddenly we had stopped. The driver opened the car door and invited us into the night, the smell of dung smoke in the air, dogs barking in an empty street. We were led into a walled building that I learned was once owned by an Italian. Dim light came from its windows. Somewhere in the distance there was a faint rhythm of drums.

We entered through a kitchen. The smell of grilled meat was strong. Four very pretty young ladies greeted us in the living room. I recognized one of them from the night I talked with Asepha at the exclusive club. She was introduced as Elizabeth.

A waiter served drinks. Kasa and his male friends ordered whiskey. He introduced the ladies as students from the university who had been chosen to host us because they spoke English. They all wore the same one-piece dress from neck to knee in different bright colors.

The ministers whom David and Sami had met during their stay had not been invited. We were introduced to two other Ethiopian men dressed in suits.

I whispered to David, "These guys must run this place. It was probably confiscated by the communist regime and given to them. They return the favor by putting together parties. Kasa never pays for anything from his own pocket."

After cocktails, we were invited to sit on cushions on the floor in front of low tables. A young lady sat next to each of us. Elizabeth didn't wait to be seated like the others. She sat down next to me and gave a shy smile. We pretended to have just met.

The meal was lamb, beef, *injera*, and vegetable salad (added to please us). We refrained from talking politics. The two Ethiopian gentlemen discoursed on Ethiopia's economy.

"Coffee is the largest crop in Ethiopia and the major foreign currency earner," said Molugeta, who was sitting at my table. "It's a strong 'Arabian'-type bean and is used for cappuccino."

"How large is Ethiopia's coffee production?"

"Ethiopian exports about $550 million in goods each year. Coffee accounts for about three hundred million of that. The other exports are leather, gold, and seed oil."

Elizabeth listened while concentrating on her food. Then, raising her eyes toward me, she said, almost in a whisper but with pride, "Coffee is an Ethiopian invention. It originated from the Kaffa region. It was first used in Ethiopia, then exported to Arabia. They called it 'produce of Kaffa.' So the name became coffee."

"So it is you Ethiopians who are responsible for this addiction we all share!"

Elizabeth laughed with delight. "That is why here in Ethiopia is the only place in the world where coffee is called *bunna*, which means 'beans.' "

MOLUGETA ROSE AND suggested that we all go upstairs for an aperitif and *bunna*. David and I both had to use the bathroom and were directed down a dim hall off the dining room. David opened a door, thinking it was a bathroom. Inside the room there was a mattress on the floor covered with a thin blanket. An old man lay on it with a beautiful young woman. Only then did we realize the game we were supposed to play. The women were available to us. It was like a scene from *A Thousand and One Nights*. Atmosphere, drinks, beautiful women. David was bewildered. "What's going on?" he asked.

"This is Ethiopia."

"In Arabia they took me to see belly dancers. But this is way beyond that. I had no idea."

"It's very deceptive," said Sami, when he heard David's report. "The women dress very conservatively. They behave like ladies. They never gave a hint of this sort of thing."

"It is as my Amharic teacher told me," I said. "In Ethiopia, sex is a private affair."

Neither David nor Sami was interested in this part of the evening. We had drinks and coffee upstairs. Again, Elizabeth sat with me. I tried to be nice to her, and, at the end of the evening, I slipped a hundred-birr note in her purse. She gave me a radiant smile.

The Londoners did, indeed, do a *mitzvah*. That month, January, saw a record number of Beta Israel emigrate—1,038.

TWENTY-SEVEN

THE FALLING HOUSE

The "honeymoon" the Londoners left behind in Addis didn't last long. February brought a new tension. On February 3, Micha Feldman and Avi Mizrahi from the Jewish Agency informed me that visa applications were being returned and Mirsha was refusing to accept new ones.

On February 5, I was called by both the foreign minister and Kasa to lodge a protest against negative coverage of the Mengistu regime in the Israeli media. Kasa had lived in Israel and knew that the government had absolutely no influence on the Israeli press. He called me to his office and began by chewing me out.

"You Israelis are ungrateful," he said. "Aren't you satisfied with the flow of emigrants? There were more than a thousand in January, double the number we agreed upon last year."

I showed some temper myself. "I'm frustrated, Kasa. When I came to Addis four months ago there were twenty-two thousand BI refugees. Today, there are twenty-two thousand BI refugees. I am becoming an ambassador of a permanent refugee camp! Births and newcomers take the place of those who emigrate."

I noticed he liked what I said. He could use this information with Mengistu and other ministers who might fear they were running out of Falashas and, with them, their clout.

A week passed and still Mirsha refused to accept new visa forms. Kasa called me to his office again. He hardly greeted me. "Asher, I am becoming a laughingstock in the government. Your feckless government isn't helping the situation. Let me show you something." He opened a door to a closet and pulled on a light. A large map of Ethiopia was mounted on the closet wall.

"Asher," he began, "a rebel offensive started a week ago, led by Tigreans who attacked us on four fronts simultaneously. Two columns of Tigreans are advancing from the west—one to Gondar and the other to Gojam. They are advancing in Shawa province from the north. From the east, two columns of Eritreans are moving toward Assab, Addis's only port." Then he added with a sad and pleading voice: "The Sudanese and the Libyans are supplying arms. Veteran Eritrean fighters are training the growing rebel army." He closed the closet door. "This information is strictly confidential. Only the high command has it." He sat next to me. "The rebels believe you have been helping Mengistu's regime, and you know what that means for the Falashas. They may be perceived as the enemy."

I was very attentive and gave him a sympathetic look, but I kept quiet. I wanted to see how far he would go. He jumped up: "Our situation is dire. Without immediate help the army will have trouble keeping control. I must go to Israel immediately to ask for arms or any other help we can get!"

I let him stew. "Kasa," I finally said. "We've been defending ourselves from Iraqi Scuds. We're also absorbing hundreds of thousands of immigrant Soviet Jews. It isn't an opportune moment to visit. But I promise to relay your message to my government."

Kasa sighed, realizing going to Israel wasn't an option. I raised the issue of the so-called flawed applications: "Mirsha has refused to take new visa applications. This is a serious matter. It contradicts commitments you made to the American representative Herman Cohen at the tripartite meeting of last November. This can create bad publicity in the United States."

"Are you threatening me?"

"Not at all. I am describing reality."

He tossed a pile of forms on the table. "See for yourself the sloppy work of Jewish Agency officials on these applications."

When I checked the forms, the objections were ridiculous. For instance, the form asked the applicant: single, married, or other. If the applicant stated that he was married, the form was returned as inadequate because the applicant didn't write the wife's name. If he wrote the name of his wife, the form was returned again with the question, "Is she working?" and again, "Was she married before?" and so on.

All this information wasn't really required, and, in any case, it wasn't asked for on the form. Nevertheless, I set Hilda to work (she had returned to Addis after the Gulf War) "correcting" the applications with Avi.

THE SITUATION AT the front as described by Kasa was worse than I thought. I went to the Mercato the next day with Konata to talk with my contacts: two females who owned textile shops and a male owner of a *teff* shop. The Mercato was a sorry place compared to what it had been only a few weeks before. It was desolate, the atmosphere sober. There were hardly any new goods; rats ran around in the garbage. Konata told me that he heard that hyenas came down from the hills and ruled the place at night. I heard stories of deserters and officers selling weaponry—even tanks—to the rebels.

The diplomatic community had been gathering intelligence on the rebels. Its two major groups were the Eritrean Peoples Liberation Front (EPLF) and Tigrean Peoples Liberation Front (TPLF). The EPLF controlled all of Eritrea except the Asmara-Keren enclave. They wanted secession. The TPLF controlled the entire province of Tigray, with its small population of three and a half million people. When the TPLF advanced beyond its territory, it incorporated other rebel movements and changed its name to Ethiopian Peoples Revolutionary Democratic Front (EPRDF). The two rebel groups had a common intermediate goal—to depose Mengistu's regime.

THE REBELS' "February Offensive" was launched, so it was assumed, to improve their military position on the ground and gain a better bargaining position in the upcoming U.S.-sponsored London talks. But to everyone's surprise, the rebels met little resistance, and that inspired them to advance farther than they had originally planned.

The Eritrean rebels from the east were approaching the main highway that connected Addis with the port of Assab. Cut the highway and imports to Addis would cease. It seemed, as the month wore on, that the Tigreans had stopped their advance toward Addis because they were overextended. With fifty thousand recruits, mostly young teenagers, Addis's three million inhabitants were too much for them to swallow. They didn't have to take Addis by force; rather, they could put it under siege and wait for its inhabitants to revolt against Mengistu.

Seeing their success, the rebels asked to postpone the London conference to May. Toward the fourth week of February, foreign embassies were evaluating the deterioration of the military situation. I went to see Angeletti.

He was as gracious as ever. But, I noticed, he did not break out the cognac. "Yes, we are going to evacuate nonessential staff, close the school, and send the children back to Italy." It was the same in other Western embassies.

The Israeli community in Addis had brought no children with them to Addis, except David's eight-year-old daughter. The five wives who had accompanied their husbands were all volunteer teachers at the Jewish day school at the compound. The departure of the Israeli teachers wasn't easy. They were attached to their Falasha students and prided themselves on being the founders of this unique school.

On March 12, Addis University closed. The next day, I received a formal application for an Israeli visa for Kasa's younger daughter, Munit. The older sister was already studying at Hebrew University in Jerusalem. The next day I was baffled to receive a visa application for Mrs. Kasa Kabede, "to visit her daughter in Jerusalem." I wondered if Mengistu knew about this application. For a moment I toyed with the idea of granting these two visas on the condition that, say, exit visas were given to two thousand Falashas. But that was too dangerous. I have never gambled in a casino, let alone gambled on people's fates.

Mirsha also asked for an Israeli visa for his wife and daughter. "I will join them later," he said. Angeletti laughed when he heard this. "At my embassy it is the same," he said. "And the same at the French, English, and Canadian embassies. The Ethiopians are rattling their sabers one moment and packing their bags the next."

I had an emotional farewell dinner with Hilda. I tried to minimize the danger, but she could see for herself how things were going. Adanich had disappeared an hour earlier. She returned with a bouquet of flowers she had bought in the neighborhood. She said she was sorry that Hilda was going back to Israel. They hugged. Adanich had wet eyes, and Hilda pushed a hundred birr into her pocket. Then we sent her home. We just wanted to be alone. We consoled ourselves over dinner by talking about our sons Ari and Gideon, who had flown over from America on their way to Addis so that we could be together. That day, they had reached Cairo to connect with Ethiopia Airlines, but I had to stop them. The situation was too precarious for them to come.

After dinner, we did the dishes together. A sadness settled over us. "I wish I didn't have to go," Hilda said. I must admit that I was slightly preoccupied, and I didn't know what to say. "Why aren't the children married," she burst out suddenly.

"What do you mean?"

"I feel as though I'm living in a house, and it's falling down around me."

"Don't be so dramatic, Hilda. Everything will be fine."

She came into my arms and we held other. It was very quiet. My ingrained optimism had rubbed off on her during our marriage, and I could feel in the softening in her body that she accepted my words and believed in me.

TWENTY-EIGHT

HONDELING

Those who sow in tears reap in joy.

—Psalm 126:5

T he situation continued to deteriorate, and Kasa, Mirsha, and company kept giving us trouble with the emigration forms. Emigration had slowed to a trickle. We began to think of evacuating all the Falashas before the country collapsed.

Lubrani and Simcha Dinitz, chairman of the Jewish Agency, flew to Washington to consult with Michael Schneider, executive vice president of the Jewish Distribution Committee, and Nate Shapiro, the president of the American Association for Ethiopian Jews. Along with other American Jewish organizations (through Michael Shilo, minister at the Israeli embassy in Washington), they appealed to the White House to help evacuate all Falashas to Israel.

General Brent Scowcroft, national security adviser, agreed to send Mengistu a letter from President Bush to ask for the release of the Falashas as a humanitarian gesture. But many thought that a letter, even from Bush, would have limited influence. Dinitz put forward Nate Shapiro's choice of Senator Rudy Boschwitz as the president's emissary to personally deliver the letter.

Malcolm Hoenlein, executive vice president of the Council of Presidents of Major Jewish Organizations, advised Boschwitz to call President Bush, who, on the spot, asked Boschwitz to be his emissary. Boschwitz was an ideal choice. He had served as chairman of the Caucus for Ethiopian Jews in the Senate and worked closely with then vice president Bush on the exodus of the Falashas from Sudan in 1984 and 1985.

I felt a new level of commitment. We were coming to the end of the road. American diplomatic muscle plus American Jewish money would be enormously persuasive. I would be criticized for stressing the importance of the Americans in the events of the coming weeks—but without them, Operation Solomon, as it came to be called, would never have gotten off the ground.

AFTER A TWO-WEEK lull in the fighting, the rebels renewed their offensive, solidifying their hold on Wollega and continuing through Illubabur, controlling all four of the country's western provinces. In the east, the Eritrean advance was stopped about twenty-five miles from the port of Assab. At Shawa province in the north, fierce battles raged.

On April 19, Zimna told me that the Ethiopian embassy workers had asked to be released at 11:00 A.M. because they had been "ordered" to be home to hear Mengistu's radio address to the nation. Whoever disobeyed this order would be punished by the *kabele*, the neighborhood committee.

I called Ato Argau, deputy director general of the Ministry for Foreign Affairs, to find out what was going on. "Yes, the president will address the nation today at 2:00 P.M. All workers were released to listen to him."

"Does the president address the nation often?"

"Not really, but the situation now requires it."

This reminded me of Il Duce's speeches during my childhood. Each time he spoke, a holiday was declared.

Speculation ran wild. Would he resign? By 2:00 P.M., the streets were empty. I was in my suite with Adanich and Tadese, my Amharic teacher. Mengistu's voice was tense, but monotonous.

"He pleads innocence," Tadese said after Mengistu's address, which lasted thirty minutes.

"What do you mean? What did he say?"

"He enumerated the great achievements of the communist revolution. Only the last few minutes he talked about the subject the people wanted to hear: losses at the front. He blamed the officers who had betrayed his trust. He blamed the rebels for the failure to reach a political solution. And he announced he would convene the *shingu*"—the parliament—"on April 21 to decide the nation's course of action."

ON APRIL 21 and in the days that followed, there was open debate on the floor of the 814-member parliament. The session was broadcast live on television. Never before had speakers been allowed to address the public uncensored! People heard dissent from Mengistu's views for the first time. The city was buzzing.

Even Konata entered the fray. He had always shied away from saying anything that might be construed as political or controversial. But after Mengistu's speech, as we drove to the embassy, I noticed he was nervous and wanted to speak.

"What did you think of the speech?" I asked him.

"Sir!" he burst out. "This regime is no good. I lived near Teodros square, on the land of my grandfather. One day Mengistu built a road. He took my land, house, and garden with no compensation. In the Somali war, he took my three sons. One died. One came home without a leg. Then Mengistu took away my God, because he said communism was the new religion."

Konata had been so careful, so much at a remove until now, I realized. It was a shock to see what had been festering inside him.

THE MODERATES WON the day. To induce the rebels to sit down for a peace conference, they offered freedom of assembly and a multiparty system. Should the rebels reject these offers, then Mengistu's conservative group would have its way to continue the war. This was the first time in seventeen years that an alternative course of action, which opposed Mengistu, had been brought to floor and accepted by the *shingu*.

While parliament was in session, an important event occurred: The rebels conquered Ambo, a well-defended city just sixty miles from Addis. Ambo became a symbol of the regime's weakness and its inability to survive. We realized that total evacuation of Beta Israel would have to occur sooner rather than later. We asked Boschwitz to come posthaste.

Amnon Shahak, deputy chief of staff of the Israel Defense Forces, flew in undercover, dressed in civilian clothes, accompanied by Lubrani. Amnon scoped security at the airport and the four-mile stretch of road between the Israeli embassy and Bole airport. He wanted to be able to hold both the road and airport while a rescue operation was in progress.

Amnon, in his forties, tall, with some gray sprinkled in his brown hair, spoke softly, more like a professor than a military man. He went here and there in Addis, but for security reasons, he kept his plans to himself.

AT THE EMBASSY, we stored water, fuel, food, money, a generator, and medicine. Reinforcements were flown in from Israel to help David's expanding job. The embassy compound's surrounding walls were strengthened.

I held weekly staff meetings. After each, I sent a report to the special Emergency Committee to Save the Beta Israel. This committee worked with the Israeli government, the Jewish Agency, and the Israeli Defense Forces to develop a detailed plan for evacuation.

As we walked out of one such meeting, I teased Zimna, who had been working day and night processing application forms, helping the new emigrants who were still trickling in from the north, and making sure people got food and medical attention.

"Zimna!" I said. "Everywhere you go, there's trouble."

"I don't know why that is, but I think you're right."

"I know I'm right. You come and the country falls apart."

He laughed and then grew thoughtful. "You know, Asher. Sometimes I think my life has been full of the most amazing luck—to come to Israel, to have wonderful children, to be able to help my people, to be able to be here now, for this! But other times I feel that I've pushed and been pushed. Still, there's so much left to do, and so many problems, and so much suffering. And I wonder what I have to show for it all."

I clapped him on the back. "Well, you have my gratitude."

He nodded but still his eyes were sad.

"And Zimna, you have my friendship, too."

He put his hands on my shoulders and kissed me three times on alternating cheeks. "I know that, Asher."

BOSCHWITZ, ON HIS way to Addis, landed in Frankfurt. Lubrani flew in to brief him. But then Boschwitz received orders not to proceed to Addis. The rebel cannon were booming near the airport, and all flights to and from Addis were canceled. Ethiopia Airlines moved its hub to Djibouti.

"Will Boschwitz's mission be scrapped?" I asked Houdek.

"No. Washington has just finished coordinating with the rebels to give Boschwitz's plane a safe landing."

"It's a relief that the mission is on!"

"Have no fear, Asher. Boschwitz's plane will land in Addis on April 26."

On April 24, the White House issued a statement on Boschwitz's mission. Boschwitz planned, it said, ". . . to raise the issue of emigration of Ethiopian Jews. . . . and discuss any U.S. efforts to help resolve the internal conflict there. . . . The president has been involved in helping the Falashas in one way or another over the years. . . . The government is allowing 500–1,000 a month to emigrate . . . our concern is that this rate is too slow. . . ."

From my point of view, this was a very encouraging statement.

This time the Americans will arrive with leverage, I thought. They have a commitment to convene and take part in a peace conference, initially planned for May 15 in London with the participation of all the parties in the conflict.

But we all felt we needed something more. In frequent discussions with Houdek, we agreed that we needed a soft landing for

Mengistu and those close to him. If they could save their lives, they would cooperate.

HOUDEK RAISED THE idea of leasing a Boeing that would make two to three daily flights to Israel, evacuating all the Falashas in ten to fifteen days. "But such a mass exodus is tricky," he said, "because the moderate Arab states will make a fuss."

I had other ideas. In phone conversations with Lubrani and Divon in Jerusalem, we came up with an alternate plan.

"We want total evacuation in two to three days," I said. "Let the Arabs be angry for a shorter period. Let's get the Falashas out before anyone knows what's happened. And we have to do it before the peace conference convenes on May 15."

I was afraid that the conference would fail—Mengistu's regime was too weak; it verged on collapse. Why should the rebels capitulate?

"It's true," Houdek said. "This conference is for show."

"We are diplomats. We can still hope for a political solution."

"I don't know if you can pull it off," said Houdek of the plan for quick evacuation. But he said he would discuss the idea with Boschwitz.

ON LANDING, BOSCHWITZ was whisked away to see Mengistu. The next day he visited me at the Israeli embassy, accompanied by Houdek; Irwin Hicks, the deputy assistant secretary of state for the Horn of Africa; and Bob Frasure of Scowcroft's staff. After a general report on our activities on behalf of Beta Israel, I took Rudy to see the miserable condition of the Falashas in Addis.

We drove north through the city, turning off the main road into a warren of twisted alleys lined with hovels. The city opened up a bit; there were small fields, littered with trash; a dusty wind blew through the dry trees. We came to a house of crumbling concrete. A low door was covered with a rag cloth; on a dirt floor kids with swollen bellies lethargically sat.

This would have been bad enough, but we went behind the house to a cowshed that had been rented to the Falasha family. They were encamped on a layer of grass that had been spread over the earth, ripe with manure. The smell was terrible; the flies were huge and persistent. There was no running water or electricity. They looked hopeless and helpless.

The sight shook Boschwitz.

"Senator," I said, "we all pray that like Moses you will take the Israelites out of Ethiopia to the Promised Land."

"I will do my best to get them out of this pigsty," Boschwitz said.

AN HOUR LATER I received a call from Kasa: "Asher, Boschwitz's visit is going well. We will expedite departure of nine thousand emigrants whose visa application forms have been completed in a matter of weeks."

"We want all the 16,500 Beta Israel left in Addis excavated not in weeks but in forty-eight hours."

There was a stunned silence on the line. "Only you Israelis could attempt such an impossible feat," Kasa finally said. "I believe that nine thousand is the number left in Addis, and besides, you are really insensitive to our relations with moderate Arab states and our large Muslim community."

"Numbers are a matter of fact. So let's talk about the departure of all Beta Israel left in Addis."

• • •

HOUDEK CALLED LATE that night: "Boschwitz made great progress. In his meeting with the president, Mengistu talked for three hours straight about the wonderful contributions he's made to the Ethiopian people. It was torture. And Boschwitz was jet-lagged! I don't know how he kept his eyes open. Then Mengistu wanted to know all about the weaponry we had used in the Gulf War. He was particularly interested in our heat-seeking missiles. Anyway, we finally got down to business. The government agreed to let the Falashas go under three conditions. One, that the operation be clandestine. Two, that Ethiopia Airlines (idle because of the war) carry out the flights—charging us full airfare for every Falasha—with Israeli backup. Three, that Ethiopia be given a 'generous financial contribution.' The third condition is really a sort of blackmail that Israel has to negotiate and take care of by herself, without American intervention."

The next morning, Kasa nailed me with one of his now famous breakfast calls.

"Why don't you just come over for breakfast," I said. "You always catch me when I'm eating."

"What a nice offer. I have fond memories of the wonderful breakfasts I had in Israel."

"Can I tempt you with toast, jam, and some very nice cheese?"

"Some other time. Listen, everything is going well with Boschwitz's mission. We want to make quick progress to implement the agreement. So can you please give me an estimate for the cost to bring a Falasha from Gondar to Addis, maintain him in Addis for twelve months, and fly him to Israel."

It took me a minute to understand the sinister thinking behind this inquiry.

• • •

PETER JACKSON OF the American Association for Ethiopian Jews had arrived in Addis to see what kind of agreement Boschwitz would wring from Mengistu. The American Jewish community was concerned about the fate of every Jew in the world—and they had a special, long-standing interest in the Falashas.

I had just finished breakfast and was getting ready to go out to Konata when an agitated Jackson ran into my suite. Jackson, an AAEJ volunteer activist on behalf of the Beta Israel, was a businessman in his fifties from Chicago.

"Kasa just summoned me into his office," he said. "He asked me, point-blank, how much American Jews were willing to pay for delivering 17,500 Ethiopian Jews directly to Israel in leased planes."

"What did you tell him?"

"I told him that we're a volunteer organization. We don't have that kind of money. And besides, Jews don't like negotiating over Jewish bodies."

"He thinks this is Ceauşescu's Romania, where the Jewish Agency paid a thousand dollars a head for Jews."

"I told Kasa that he should be careful of giving the impression that Ethiopia was 'trading Jews for money.' We are very sensitive to this attitude. Then he asked me to find out for him if there is American government money for this project. When he led me out of his office, he whispered, 'Don't call me from the ambassador's suite or the embassy. Those lines are tapped.' "

"I don't know why he thinks it's such a secret. Sometimes we send messages to Kasa through the tapped phone. My suite is bugged, too. That's why we're standing on the terrace."

"Oh!"

"Did you report this to Houdek?"

"I told him the whole story. Kasa also asked me to estimate the cost of bringing a Falasha from Gondar to Addis and allocating him housing, food, health care, and clothing for twelve months. Then he said, add incidental expenses such as flying in Israeli social workers, doctors, nurses, and Jewish Agency workers who deal with passports, visas, and air tickets. Add air travel to Israel via Rome and expenses during their stay while in transit in Rome. And then add the Ethiopian government's expenses on the Falashas in Gondar, such as health, school, police to keep order, and so forth."

I had to laugh. Kasa was really too much. "The whole thing is a charade," I said. "If people's lives weren't at stake it would be ludicrous. But given the situation, it's an outrage. The last estimate is absurd! The Beta Israel were like slaves—first to the landlords and later to the government. They never had clinics, health care, or government education. The JDC and Jewish Agency opened schools for the Beta Israel in Asmara, Gondar, and Addis, which non–Beta Israeli children enjoyed. But please, Mr. Jackson, don't despair. There is a bright side to your story. Ethiopia is ready for a deal! That's what counts."

ULTIMATELY, JACKSON CAME back to Kasa and gave him the estimated expenses for all 17,500 Falashas—he tallied it at seventeen to twenty million dollars, out of which twelve million was airfare. Kasa accepted the estimate as reasonable.

A day later, Jackson visited me again and told me that he had made a secret deal to pay Kasa two hundred dollars for every Beta Israel. Payment would be transferred after every plane that landed in Israel. That got me worried.

"This agreement leaves you open to blackmail," I said. "Kasa

will let half go and then up the price. I have no authority to interfere on how you spend your money. But I vehemently oppose
payment by planeload."

I asked him to change the agreement to say that payment
would be delivered only after the last Falasha had left Ethiopian
soil and landed in Israel. An hour later, Jackson came back and
confirmed the change.

FOUR DAYS PASSED and nothing moved. Statements by Tesfaye
Dinka, the prime minister, and Wolde Selassie, minister of the
interior, that they would intervene in the Beta Israel issue came to
nothing. Kasa ferociously guarded his turf, and he was able to
derail even a strong coalition of two prominent cabinet members.

On April 30, a nervous Houdek came to the embassy. "Asher,
what happened to you Israelis? Did you decide you don't want to
rescue the Falashas? I heard BBC news and read in the *Jerusalem
Post* about the animosity you feel toward the regime whose help
you seek. This, at a critical moment in negotiations, and after
their explicit request to keep the operation confidential."

What now, I thought. "I'm sorry, I hadn't heard . . ." I said,
rather lamely, to Houdek.

"How can you not have seen this?" He waved a newspaper in
front of me.

"What! I haven't seen it."

"Let me read to you. 'The Israelis are very worried about the
fate of the sixteen thousand BI in Addis . . . there is danger they
will be caught in the cross fire of the civil war . . . the Jewish
Agency is making preparations to absorb a flow of Beta Israel
immigrants to Israel . . . Mengistu's regime is collapsing . . . Israel
has offered Mengistu political asylum for emigration of all BI to
Israel . . .'"

"This is terrible," I said. "I don't know what happened."

There was uproar. I won't bore you with the list of calls I got in protest. I spoke to Jerusalem. Kasa, of course, wanted an explanation.

I apologized profusely and asked for time to plug the leak. I got word that the story had originated in England. Suddenly, I recalled that Peter Jackson had told me that when he met with Kasa the day before, they were interrupted by a phone call that Kasa put off, saying, "Call me tomorrow at this time and I will give you the interview in English." He was so devious! The timetable was speeding up; Kasa was getting unsatisfactory results, feeling for bribes, so he created a grievance to slow things down. In a moment of intuition, which first amazed and then nauseated me, I knew that Kasa himself was the leak! But I never said a word. What was the point? It would have infuriated him and jeopardized the mission.

To better secure ourselves, the ministry convened all newspaper editors and by consent all agreed to keep this issue out of the press until after the Beta Israel exodus from Ethiopia. For Israel this was an extraordinary event. I called Kasa to tell him that we had managed to muzzle the press.

"Well done, Asher," he said.

I think he really was impressed.

TWENTY-NINE

THE ESCAPE

Modalities is a terrible word in diplomacy. It means nothing and everything, and I would be very glad if I never had to hear it again. I got a stomach full of "shifting modalities" in the aftermath of Boschwitz's mission as the deal he made changed, unraveled, was put back together, amended, delayed, and changed yet again.

Lubrani wanted to come from Jerusalem to handle negotiating the payment to the government, but Kasa said no. On May 4, the Ethiopian embassy in Israel refused to grant entry visas to two Jewish Agency officers and Divon. I protested. Kasa insisted that the Lubrani and Divon trips should be postponed until Ethiopia was ready to negotiate. What was holding them up? I called Houdek, who said the Ethiopians were waiting to receive the official invitation from the United States to participate in the London peace conference. Then they would address the issue of the Falashas.

Kasa allowed Lubrani to land on May 8. Marathon meetings commenced. Eighty-five to one hundred million dollars was the deal Kasa laid on the table—the airlift, in secret, to be executed over the course of two to three days. Lubrani suggested that Israeli planes perform the operation and offered twenty-five to thirty million. Houdek, outraged at the amount, said "it smelled of blackmail." The United States feared that Mengistu would use it to buy arms.

Negotiations with Kasa were nerve-racking. He made an appointment but failed to show up. He would suddenly appear at the Hilton, pat my back, and say, "I have been looking for Uri all morning without success. But now I am in a hurry. I will call in the evening." Did he call? Of course not! He wanted to break our will, hoping we would give in to whatever he asked.

I felt sure he had sold himself to his bosses—that he was under pressure from his side to deliver a certain amount of money. There were complexities at work that Lubrani and I only glimpsed.

On May 10, the Americans sent word that the rebels had requested pushing back the London peace conference to May 27. Lubrani asked that the Americans tell Mengistu that the conference was being postponed due to the lack of resolution of the Falasha issue. We were fighting fire with fire.

Eight days and five meetings later, the money issue had still not been resolved. After his psychological warfare failed, Kasa used several arm-twisting tactics; the most outrageous was the threat to draft male Falashas into the Ethiopian army—or what was left of it.

When all this didn't help, Kasa suggested "splitting the difference." You say $30 million, we say $85 million—what about $62.5 million? Lubrani said no.

It was our turn to put Kasa to the test. This was one of the times we sent him a message through my tapped telephone. We announced loudly that Lubrani had failed in his mission and would fly back to Israel the following day. It worked! Just when we were leaving for the airport, the phone rang. Kasa requested a meeting at the airport and had a new offer: fifty million. Lubrani refused again, but suggested that perhaps a personal note from President Bush, praising Ethiopia's humanitarian gesture, might close the gap. Kasa was speechless.

To throw off criticism, Kasa led a rumor campaign among foreign diplomats and journalists. Israel was not interested in Falasha emigration, he said. That was why the negotiations were dragging. The Falashas felt unwelcome in Israel. They were not really interested in emigrating. That same week I organized visits by most of the ambassadors to the embassy compound to see the Falashas' improved condition and to hear them say, "We want to go to Jerusalem." Kasa's tactics boomeranged. Now the ambassadors all asked him what was holding up emigration.

AFTER LUBRANI'S DEPARTURE, it was our turn to squeeze. Houdek called Kasa and told him that he had just lost thirty million dollars, the goodwill of Israel and the United States, and, maybe, the London peace conference. Houdek exaggerated—we knew the Americans would host the London peace conference anyway—but we wanted to shake Kasa and pressure him into a deal.

It was May 17, and we had just a ten-day window of opportunity to extract the Falashas before all hell broke loose. The rebels' motivation to attend the peace conference was diminishing by the minute. Only pressure from the United States was inducing them to participate.

Mengistu, at this stage, was an enigma. We did not have face-to-face meetings with him. Was he preparing to make a stand at the palace with his remaining ten thousand elite soldiers—or brooding alone in a hideaway?

On May 16, the rebels surged forward on all fronts, conquering Dessie, Debre Birhan, Ginji, and recapturing Ambo. Addis was now under siege. That same day the rebels sent a message through the Americans, asking Israel to make all efforts to evacuate the Falashas from the capital. They preferred to have this problem behind them, but if the emigration didn't materialize, they promised to protect them. They asked us to gather the Falashas in one area. They feared lawlessness and mob rule.

We pressed for time. Lubrani had intensive meetings with Prime Minister Yitzhak Shamir. We decided to kick in another few million. We would offer thirty-five million dollars to the Ethiopians, in order not to offend their pride. It was at this point that the deal and evacuation were dubbed "Operation Solomon."

KASA NOW ASKED me to invite Lubrani to Addis. He flew in early on the morning of May 21. We consulted in my suite: Should we try to negotiate directly with Mengistu to reach a final decision quickly?

No sooner had we said the name *Mengistu* than the telephone rang. Houdek was on the line: "Asher, Mengistu left early this morning for an unknown destination. He appointed Gebre Kidan as acting president."

Houdek had to repeat this twice for me to grasp it.

Later we learned that on the morning of May 21, Mengistu had summoned his three most senior officials, Vice President Tesfaye Gebre Kidan, Interior Minister Tesfaye Wolde Selassie, and Prime Minister Tesfaye Dinka to meet him at Bole airport (they were known as the "Three Tesfayes"). There, with the plane's engine running, he informed the shocked trio that he was leaving Ethiopia so as not to be an impediment to a "political settlement."

Apparently, after this announcement, Mengistu walked away to a small jet plane and took off with seven members of his clan. Just like that he ended his seventeen years in power. And this was a ruler who had reputedly never walked away from a fight.

LATER WE LEARNED that his escape had been planned in advance. Robert Mugabe, the president of Zimbabwe, offered him asylum, repaying a debt for the help Mengistu had given him when Zimbabwe was struggling against the British for independence.

Mugabe would refuse again and again the rebel government's request for Mengistu's extradition to stand trial for atrocities committed during his rule. He and his clan were granted permanent residence in Zimbabwe—and he was given a Zimbabwe diplomatic passport to provide further immunity for him on his travels for medical treatment to South Africa. Ethiopia's last request for his extradition, in 2001, was again rejected. Mugabe admitted: "Yes, he has committed crimes, but he is now a political refugee and is entitled to rights as such."

IN MY SUITE on that morning of May 21, we considered our next step. Did Kasa have the authority to negotiate without Mengistu's backing? The Boschwitz-Mengistu agreement was concluded in an orderly fashion, with the participation of the most important leadership. We assumed that Kasa could proceed with the agreement regardless. In any case, we should be able to learn from Kasa what was really happening in the government.

Lubrani left at 11:45 A.M. for Kasa's office. At 1:00 P.M., the radio announced publicly that their president had left the country (without saying why or where) and that Gebre Kidan was acting president. How would people react? Would they take the law into their own hands? Would they begin burning and looting? There were tens of thousands of armed soldiers, deserters roaming the streets without pay, money, or a decent place to sleep. Would they run amok?

David called from the embassy: "I'm concerned. But so far I haven't noticed anything unusual. The Beta Israel neighborhoods are quiet. But the situation could change at any time. Let's keep in touch."

At 1:30 P.M. there was still no word from Lubrani. Had he been taken hostage? I broke out in a cold sweat and dialed Kasa's number. His secretary assured me that they were having coffee. And indeed, shortly after, Lubrani returned with a deal—complete emigration before May 27. We could use Israeli planes, except for one token Ethiopia Airlines flight. The generous contribution? Thirty-five million dollars.

THE NEW GOVERNMENT had a hard time dealing with the rapid sequence of events: the peace conference, the rebels at the gate of Addis, the deserters, poor, hungry, and desolate, and, above all, Mengistu's ten thousand elite soldiers in the palace.

It was fortunate that General Gebre Kidan was in charge. He was respected and had proved himself on the battlefield.

That afternoon, tanks roamed the streets; they took positions at the main government offices, the television and radio stations, and the main highways.

Dinka summoned Houdek and asked his help to reach a cease-fire with the rebels. He offered a transitional government in which the rebels would participate, and then free elections—all before the peace conference. Houdek promised to immediately convey this offer and then asked: "Will Kasa continue dealing with the Falashas?"

Dinka looked him in the eye. "Who is Kasa?" he said flatly.

Houdek was stunned. "Who, then, has the authority to deal with this issue?"

"Kidan."

Houdek asked for Kidan's help.

"As a military man, I don't understand this issue," Kidan said.

Houdek briefed him and mentioned Kasa as the expert on this issue. Kidan was contemptuous. "He doesn't make decisions," Kidan said.

Houdek persisted. "Let Kasa give you the data. You make the decision."

IT WAS NOW obvious that Kasa did not have the authority to conclude an agreement with Lubrani. Houdek's intervention gave Kasa the chance to reclaim responsibility in a situation upon which his future depended, both his life and his status. Kasa rushed to the new government to tell them the terms he had negotiated with Lubrani and to try to get their approval. Wolde Selassie said yes, Dinka said yes, but insisted that the operation take place after May 27 to ensure that the United States would continue to help in the negotiations with the rebels.

Kidan said yes to the airlift before May 27, contingent upon receiving a personal request from President Bush, so as to eliminate internal criticism. Newly elected, he couldn't go before the politburo and assume responsibility for the decision. This way he could say: Look, the Americans are sponsoring the conference, we need them, so let's give the Israelis the Falashas.

Bush's note became very important. His response was immediate and arrived by fax on May 22. In it, he repeated the U.S. commitment to convene the peace conference in London and reminded Kidan of Ethiopia's positive response to Boschwitz's request "for the expeditious departure of all remaining Falashas to Israel."

The clock started ticking. Would we make it? It is said that time is too swift for those who fear, too long for those who suffer, too short for those who rejoice, but too slow for those who wait. Time for us began to move in slow motion.

IPSO FACTO

Once we knew that we could get the Beta Israel out in one operation, preparations began. We formed a committee headed by Director General Reuven Merhav with representatives from the Foreign Ministry, the Israeli air force, and the Jewish Agency.

The agency's task was twofold: organize the embassy in Addis for the departure of the Ethiopians to Israel, and absorb the fifteen thousand people who would land in Israel with nothing except the clothes on their backs.

We knew how many Falashas were in Addis by the registration at the embassy for monthly stipends. But we knew we could be mistaken by 2 or 3 percent either way.

The agency planned to vacate most absorption centers throughout Israel and rent thirty-two hotels. They prepared to register the immigrants on landing, provide transportation for the hundreds of people on every plane that landed, and feed them, because they would arrive without having eaten for many hours.

At the embassy, we were faced with the task of gathering fifteen thousand people scattered around Addis into the embassy compound on short notice—two to four hours. For this plan, Kobi Friedman of the Jewish Distribution Committee and his team resorted to the model of the network of the Jewish underground in pre-Israel days.

Friedman appointed lieutenants. Each lieutenant was responsible for ten or more families. Every ten lieutenants had a captain and every ten or more captains had a commander responsible for one of five areas in which the Falashas lived. These five commanders had to report to "Adisu the General," who worked under Friedman. The system was tested twice and both times it worked well—we could gather all the Falashas in the embassy compound in less than three hours.

Micha Feldman, Avi Mizrahi, and Zimna Berhane received the Falashas in the embassy compound. On arrival, they were directed to the school area. They had to present their embassy-issued ID card, and their identity was checked. They crossed to a second area, organized by family. Father, mother, and children had to be together. If one was missing, the family had to wait until he arrived. Numbers were pasted on the children's foreheads for easy identification. Then family units crossed to the third area, where buses were waiting to take them to the airport.

We hired buses from every possible source. The drivers were paid handsomely to work as many hours as necessary. The distance from the embassy to the airport was almost four miles. An hour was allocated for the round trip. At the airport, space was readied for three thousand people at one time.

Patients in hospitals were registered and recorded by the doctors. A special medical team would evacuate them on a hospital plane.

Because of the lack of gasoline in Addis, our planes would have to carry enough fuel for the round-trip—Tel Aviv to Addis to Tel Aviv.

Initially, the planning teams considered other options for evacuation, such as using another airport and even evacuation by land to Kenya. But all were discarded as too risky. We also wanted to ensure that we carried out the operation with the Ethiopian government's consent and cooperation.

The atmosphere in Addis was tense. Tanks roamed the streets. Sometimes we heard shooting by day, but nobody knew who was shooting at whom. Were we seeing government or rebel tanks? The shooting escalated at night and came from all directions. We assumed that residents were shooting to repulse invaders or thieves.

It was like the American Wild West. Adanich came to the suite crying that a man in a crowded bus had stolen five birr from her and escaped at the next stop. Two men, who were after his wallet, attacked Friedman in the market. He kicked the first and grabbed the other. The thief slipped out of his jacket and escaped. Friedman presented the jacket to a Beta Israel man.

Houdek said marine reinforcements had arrived. General Schwarzkopf, the commander during the Gulf War, had offered to send helicopters to evacuate the American embassy staff to Saudi Arabia. "You and yours are welcome to join us," Houdek said. I thanked him, without mentioning the problematic situation for me, as Israeli ambassador, of landing in Saudi Arabia.

Angeletti, the Italian ambassador, said that Italian warships on their return home from the Gulf War were given orders to stand by in the sea off Ethiopia for a few days until the situation was clarified. He, too, offered his help. So did other friendly countries.

It felt good to have these options, but I relied on David and his two colleagues who had flown into Addis. David was levelheaded and inspired confidence.

At the same time, the JDC made arrangements with other UN organizations in Addis to look after the Beta Israel in case the Israeli embassy's staff had to be evacuated.

On May 23, there were just three days left for the operation. The window of opportunity narrowed by the hour. At 11:00 A.M., Lubrani and I went to see Houdek at the U.S. embassy. He said he hadn't been given the green light for Operation Solomon from Kidan, the acting president. Konata then dropped me at the Italian embassy for an appointment with Angeletti and drove Lubrani to the Hilton. When I stepped into the embassy, Angeletti ran over to me excitedly. "Your secretary has called three times in the last hour because Ato Argau of the Foreign Ministry is looking for you most urgently."

While he was talking, he led me to the telephone on his desk. I called Argau. He sounded rushed. "I have been looking for you for the last hour," he said.

"I am sorry, but here I am."

"Tesfaye Tadesse, the newly appointed foreign minister has an urgent message for you. Come as quickly as possible."

"I will be there."

But I had no car. Angeletti saw my despair and called his driver: "Take the ambassador to the Foreign Ministry quickly and cover the Italian flag!"

"*Mille grazie!*" I said, and I was out the door.

• • •

"I HAVE INSTRUCTIONS." Tadesse ushered me into his office. "We passed a resolution this morning to allow the exodus of all Falashas to Israel before May 27. Logistics must be coordinated with the minister of the interior. And the operation must be kept confidential, out of consideration for the moderate Arab states friendly to Ethiopia."

A surge of relief and then excitement washed through me. I was overwhelmed. I felt that I had won the lottery. My breath came faster. We had been waiting and pushing for so long. Now, we had finally been handed the ball and told, "Run!"

MY SUITE BECAME the hub of Operation Solomon. Everyone was there. Adanich ran to and fro, preparing snacks and drinks. Merhav called. We decided that Solomon would begin the following morning, Friday, May 24. It was now or never!

I called the minister of the interior, but there was no answer. I called every number that appeared in the telephone book, but no one was there. Already, during my meeting with Tadesse, I had sensed that the government offices were empty.

We called a meeting of all the embassy staff and told them the operation was on. Energy crackled in the room. Each branch at the embassy—JDC, Jewish Agency, security—sat with its team to rehearse their tasks. Mirsha, deputy minister of the interior, called and told me to come to him at 4:00 P.M. I took David and Maimon. Konata drove. Since his outburst after Mengistu's speech, he had closed back into himself. He, like most other Ethiopians, had no idea what was coming, but whatever it was it could hardly be worse than what they had endured under the derg.

The few people in the streets walked quickly, faces down, looking as if they had only one thing in mind—to rush home. The area
in front of the Interior Ministry's building, normally full of people
applying for passports and visas, was completely empty. Inside, the
building was deserted. On the second floor, only Mirsha was in his
office with a very frightened secretary who did not understand
why was she forced to be there at such a dangerous time.

Mirsha was seated behind his desk. "We can't let the operation
go forward. Rebels have entered the city. The government's
forces are losing control."

I didn't let this dissuade me. "My instructions are to proceed. I
am here to coordinate details."

He raised his head. "Then why don't you stop the rebel
advance?"

I had always preferred to work with Mirsha. He was not complicated; I did not have to be on guard with him. He said what he
meant and spoke to the point. Unlike Kasa, I always knew where I
stood with him. Sometimes when I complained about his office's
performance or lack of it, he would say, "Take this up with Kasa,"
a hint that he had to follow Kasa's instructions and that he was not
always comfortable with his orders.

Once I invited him to dinner with Amnon Mantver, director
general of the Jewish Agency. Toward the end of the evening he
told Mantver a story about his grandmother who, he said, used to
light two candles every Friday evening, and that only lately had
he realized that these must have been from an old Jewish tradition
of Sabbath candles. He well knew that a Jewish grandparent entitled the grandson to the right of immigration to Israel. I could see
that he hoped this cooperation with us would secure his future,
indeed his life.

Mirsha called around to assess the situation, but no one
answered. Had we lost the opportunity? The rebels had explicitly

said that they would not enter Addis before the opening of the peace conference on May 27. That was on Monday, three days hence. We needed only two days, Friday and Saturday.

I called Houdek, who told me that the rebels were four miles from the city, but he asked me to let him check again. Five minutes later he called back: "I hear that the rebels are in the Mercato. But the problem is that the information keeps changing. I will call back."

I did not share Houdek's information with Mirsha. I was afraid he would walk away. Maimon asked me in Hebrew if it was wise to ignore the rebel takeover of the city. I told him the news was hearsay because nobody knew for certain what was going on. In any case we had until the next morning to cancel if the situation warranted.

I gave Mirsha the list of things we needed for the operation:

- To let us secure and guard the road from the embassy to the airport.

- To allow us to operate through the night during the curfew.

- To clear one area, the northeast corner of the airport, for our operation.

- To inform the airport controller of the operation and have an Israeli air force officer with him to help communicate with the pilots.

"The Israeli planes will start landing tomorrow at 10:00 A.M.," I said. He raised his head, his glasses fell on the desk, and his mouth fell open: "Let us hope. I am a religious man." And he looked at me as if I was crazy.

• • •

THE SECRETARY CONTINUED phoning, trying to contact the people who would work with us the next day, but no one was around. Then Kasa called. "I'm coming to your suite," he said and hung up. We all jumped into my car; Mirsha, too. Konata sped through the empty streets to the Hilton.

Lubrani, Kasa, Mirsha, Ami Bergman from the JDC, Micha Feldman, and others were gathered in my suite. Houdek called as I walked through the door. "The information about the Beta Israel exodus has been transmitted to the rebels," he said. "They promised they would neither interfere with nor disrupt the operation."

At this news all felt a surge of joy. We were then able to plan the details of the operation with more certainty.

Mirsha's difficult problem was to prepare passports and visas for fifteen thousand Beta Israel so that the Ethiopian emigration officers at the airport would let them go. Under normal circumstances, the Interior Ministry could issue one hundred passports daily. Even if the ministry workers showed up the next day, how could they issue fifteen thousand in a matter of hours?

"I can't allow Ethiopian citizens to leave the country without passports!" said Mirsha. After a heated discussion, he had to accept Feldman's suggestion. The Jewish Agency would give a list of all Beta Israel to be handed over to the emigration authority at the airport. The same list would allow Mirsha to issue passports ipso facto—that is, after the operation. Of course they never did. This list gave Mirsha a fig leaf for the exodus without passports.

Mirsha arranged Addis police support, so we could operate after curfew at 9:00 P.M. He also arranged for an Israeli air force officer to work with an Ethiopian air controller.

At 11:00 P.M. we had completed the list of requests and made an appointment to meet in Mirsha's office at 7:30 the following morning to make sure everything was set.

Just then, Merhav called: "Operation Solomon has been given the go-ahead by the prime minister, to commence tomorrow at 10:00 A.M. It is a historic moment and you are blessed to take part in such a *mitzvah*. Shalom."

THIRTY-ONE

OPERATION SOLOMON

At 6:00 A.M. on Friday, May 24, Amir Maimon checked the route from the airport to the embassy. All was quiet; the roads were open. Kobi Friedman and Ami Bergman from JDC were asked to round up the Beta Israel at the embassy. For the first time they would be told they were going to Jerusalem.

At 7:30, I went to Mirsha's office with Maimon and David. Mirsha was alone in the building, without even a secretary. He confirmed that during the night he had reached all the people we needed for the operation and secured their cooperation.

At 8:30, we went with Mirsha to the airport and found an air traffic controller panicked by so many planes flying overhead. He knew nothing about what was going on. Mirsha straightened things out, and the northeast area of the airport was cleared for the Israeli planes.

At 10:00, two unmarked Boeings landed. One was directed to

the distant corner of the airport. Two hundred *golani*, elite commandos, disembarked. They had all volunteered for this duty. They went on the most dangerous missions. They were trained in special weapons, night fighting, communications, and hand-to-hand combat.

The *golani* would secure the route from the embassy to the airport—in case there was trouble. Their orders at that point were to stay at the airport in a state of high alert. They took up position at a corner of the runway. I was happy to note that some of the soldiers were Ethiopians who had come to Israel in earlier immigrations.

The second Boeing was a hospital plane to carry the sick and the elderly, who were to be evacuated first. The planes also carried dozens of Jewish Agency officers and a team of eight Foreign Ministry officials, including Divon.

Minutes later, two more planes landed and parked at the center of the runway. A Soviet Ilyushin was parked on the extreme right of the airport, its Russian crewmembers clearly puzzled. Why all this activity in an airport that had been idle for ten days? What was going on?

More planes appeared over the mountains to the north. The commando units made their way across the tarmac. It looked like the set of a Hollywood movie. I must admit that I was trembling—overwhelmed with emotion and pride.

AT 10:30 A.M., we drove in a convoy to the embassy. As we approached, I could see the huge size of the crowd, much more than the fifteen thousand that Feldman and Zimna had estimated. There were twenty to twenty-five thousand people—Falasha neighbors who wanted to leave with them—shouting and pushing toward the embassy gates. The buses hired to take the Beta Israel to the airport were stuck and the operation delayed. The police had to be called in to help open the road for traffic. I left the car with Konata and walked in through the crowd.

At 11:30 A.M., I received a call from Kasa, demanding a halt to the operation: "No money, no flights," he said.

Lubrani got on the line. "This isn't a James Bond film, Kasa," he said. "We don't carry thirty-five million in hundred-dollar bills in an attaché case. It's five in the morning in New York. In four hours, when the U.S. banks open, we'll wire the money."

Kasa backed off.

At 12:30 the first two buses left the compound. Slowly, with difficulty, they made their way through the crowd. People clung to their sides and clambered to their tops. The police managed to get them down.

Each forty-seat bus carried seventy to eighty people. They had no luggage. They had been told, "Come as you are. Don't bring anything except valuable religious items."

At 1:15, the first flight took off—three hundred Ethiopians aboard. By late afternoon, Operation Solomon was running smoothly.

SIMCHA DINITZ, THE chairman of the Jewish Agency, and Lubrani had raised the thirty-five million dollars in New York a month earlier. They had met with the leaders of the United Jewish Appeal (UJA), the central arm for all the major Jewish philanthropies, and explained that the money was needed to save the Jews of Ethiopia. They admitted it was a ransom, but Dinitz said we had been paying ransom to redeem Jewish lives throughout our history. Marty Kraar, executive vice president of the UJF, had called the various philanthropic groups and they raised the amount in several days.

Israel paid for the operation itself.

At 3:00 P.M., Lubrani, Kasa, and I met at my suite to settle the transfer. Kasa reported that Prime Minister Tesfaye Dinka was fuming, demanding that we stop the operation immediately. Why? BBC news was broadcasting a full and colorful report of Operation Solomon. Dinka claimed that this breached our confidentiality agreement.

"Kasa," I said, "Israel is enforcing censorship for the duration of the operation, an extreme step. But we can't be responsible for the world media."

Kasa spread his hands in a gesture of acceptance. "Touché!" he said.

Perhaps he was just tired of fighting.

WE TURNED TO the transfer of the money. Three P.M. in Addis is 9:00 A.M. New York time. After coordinating calls among Addis, Jerusalem, and the Chase Manhattan Bank in New York, it become clear that the account number Kasa had given us for the transfer wasn't an official "government of Ethiopia" account.

"I'm so sorry for the confusion," Kasa said, unfazed.

Kasa called different ministers, but nobody answered. I thought: What if we canceled the transfer? Mengistu was gone, the prime minister was packing for the London peace conference, and Kasa couldn't even locate ministers by phone. The regime was disintegrating; the London conference was doomed to fail. What moral obligation did we have to pay a commitment forced upon us under duress in the form of ransom? Moreover, the future, indeed the life of Kasa, the person in charge of blackmailing us, depended on our goodwill to throw him a lifeline at the last moment of the operation. We could assume that he wouldn't raise hell if the transfer were somehow held up for "technical reasons."

But since I wasn't directly involved in the financial negotiations with Kasa, I didn't see myself fit to present such a daring and controversial proposal. What if a minister found out and gave orders that endangered lives? Still, this thought has never stopped bothering me.

It took Kasa more than two hours to finally come up with the correct account number. We took maximum precautions to ensure that no one, but no one, except "the legal government of Ethiopia" could touch the money. It was in an account that could only be released by the State Department's confirmation of a legal and recognized government after the London peace conference. We could only hope that the money would be spent for the benefit of Ethiopia's poor.

By 6:00 P.M., when I left the Hilton and drove to the airport, more than three thousand Ethiopians had already departed (the first plane had landed at Ben-Gurion airport at 4:45). I arrived at the airport at dusk. It was a surreal scene. The Beta Israel saw their emigration to Jerusalem as an act of God, a sacred deliverance. Young and old were dressed in festive clothes, covered with *shammas*, their faces filled with reverence and awe. They marched behind Jewish Agency officers toward the planes. They looked like a walking white cloud. They were led to openings in the rear of the planes; huge doors closed behind them, and they disappeared.

They sat on the floor, very close to one another. The planes had been stripped of seats and other fittings in order to allow more space for passengers. One jumbo jet, which usually carried fewer than 500 passengers, took 1,087, a feat recorded in the *Guinness Book of Records.*

NIGHT FELL. THE buses went back and forth from the embassy. Planes landed, were filled, and took off into the night. Everyone was working nonstop. We were all filled with energy. I had caught sight of Zimna at several points during the day, but he was so busy running he barely had breath to say hello.

The *golani* were allowed to go in shifts to see what was happening at the embassy.

At some point during the evening, Houdek's car approached the tarmac. He had come to witness the result of many months of arduous negotiations. He was a seasoned diplomat in Africa. He had witnessed revolutions, famine, civil war. But the sight of the Beta Israel exodus moved him. We spontaneously embraced. From close up, I could see his eyes were moist.

WHEN I RETURNED to my suite, I found Kasa. He was sad, unfocused. He asked for a drink and I opened a bottle of Chivas. He looked like a man whose world had been destroyed; he faced an unknown future. His light gray suit was crumpled, his blue-and-white tie loose, his hair uncombed. He was attached to Ethiopia's land, culture, and religion. But he knew he had to go into exile. "If I remain here the rebels will put me to death," he said.

He sat drinking, carping on the regime's mistakes. For the first time, he spoke of "Mengistu's narrow horizon and lack of sophistication." He denied rumors that he was related to Mengistu. He dug into his pocket. "All other members of cabinet carry communist party cards, but I carry this"—he showed us a picture of the Virgin Mary. "Communism," he said, "was a tragedy for Ethiopia." He accused the rebels of being radical communists of the Albanian type. He was concerned that they would allow Eritrea to secede. "That will be the beginning of the country's disintegration," he said and hung his head.

Two hours later, Kasa had finished the Chivas, all by himself. I had never seen anything like it, except in the movies. I finally understood how he had run up such a high bar bill at the Tel Aviv Hilton.

Toward the end of the evening, he asked to be smuggled out of the country on one of the operation's flights, and to be allowed to live in Israel for a short period until he could settle elsewhere. Houdek had said that Kasa would be eligible for an American visa at a later date because there was no evidence that he had killed anyone, or given the orders to kill anyone.

Lubrani was inclined to say yes to Kasa's request. He asked me—and I had mixed feelings. Even at this hour, one never knew what harm a desperate man who was still in the government could do. So I agreed, but I stipulated that if Kasa left it had to be on the last flight, to secure the total evacuation of the Beta Israel.

Technically speaking, we followed the law. He was still part of the regime, possessed a valid passport and Israeli tourist visa for three months, and he had not asked for political asylum. Ditto for Mirsha.

At 11:25 P.M., Kasa left. He had drunk a whole bottle of whiskey, but he was steady on his feet. A few minutes later, Maimon called and informed us that 6,250 Falashas had already departed for Israel. Maimon added that during the night the process had quickened, after the curfew had gone into effect and the Ethiopian officials had gone to sleep.

Saturday, May 25, 6:30 A.M. Maimon woke me up. "We can actually finish the operation in one hour's time," he said. "There are fewer than a thousand Falashas left." But the commander of the operation, Shahak, decided to have the last two planes leave at 11:00 A.M. He wanted to make sure the Israeli teams scattered through the city and the American volunteers weren't stranded in Addis.

At 8:00 A.M., the Foreign Ministry staff gathered in my suite to determine our next step. Would there be resistance to the rebels from the ten thousand so-called elite forces at the palace? That was a big question and nobody had an answer.

Moshe Yegar suggested that due to the unstable situation and unpredictable future, all the embassy staff should be evacuated until after the war was over.

I wasn't buying that. "I don't see all hell breaking loose when the rebels storm Mengistu's palace," I said. "The rebels may have grievances about Israel helping Mengistu, but, as a new regime, they will want to establish good relations with other countries. Many hundreds of Beta Israel are still left behind in different parts of the country who were unable to come to Addis in time for the operation. Friendly relations with the new regime would gain us goodwill for future emigration."

"If the ambassador stays, I stay," said Maimon.

"I'm not leaving Asher's side," said David. "And that goes for my two security men, too."

Yegar threw up his hand. "Okay. Have it your way. But Asher, what will I say to Hilda? She will hate me for not bringing you home!"

"I know my wife. She will understand."

We arranged for the rest of the embassy staff, including Zimna, to be evacuated on the last flight.

• • •

WHILE I WAS hashing it out with Yegar, Simcha Dinitz, the chairman of the Jewish Agency and a neighbor of mine in Jerusalem, called. "Asher, don't play the hero. Take the last flight out!" he said.

I believed that I knew better. The resistance to the rebels would be short-lived. In any case, the American, Italian, and German embassies were ready to shelter my staff and me if the situation warranted it.

At 10:30 P.M., Konata drove me to the airport to bid farewell to all the staff who had taken part in Operation Solomon: the Jewish Agency, JDC, IDF, Lubrani, and my colleagues from the Foreign Ministry.

Just minutes before the last plane boarded, two Ethiopian women who were escorting a Falasha family were stopped by a Jewish Agency official and told that they were not entitled to immigrate to Israel. This happened right on the tarmac. The scene quickly went from talking to shouting, then from shouting to crying. The two women threw themselves on the ground and began beating themselves. The Beta Israel woman emerged from the plane and clung to the Ethiopian women, shouting, "Either we all go or nobody goes!" This went on for almost ten minutes. The pilot didn't want the flight disrupted, so he ordered the Jewish Agency man to let all three women board. Minutes later, the last plane was in the sky.

OPERATION SOLOMON STARTED on Friday, May 24, at 10:00 A.M. and ended on Saturday, May 25, at 11:00 A.M.—it lasted exactly twenty-five hours.

In all, 14,200 immigrants were carried from Addis to Ben-Gurion airport. Thirty-five military and civilian planes made forty-one flights. At one point, there were twenty-eight planes in the air.

The distance each plane traveled was fifteen hundred miles, and the flight lasted about four hours.

The Israeli air force had worked six weeks preparing for the operation under Commander Elihu Ben-Nun. Several times the pilots had been in the cockpits, switched on their engines, but had to abort at the last minute.

The planes were already airborne *before* the final green light.

There were no mishaps or accidents. The planes flew without insignia because they passed close to enemy territory.

One hundred forty immigrants needed medical attention. Among them were ten women who gave birth to eleven children from the time they were at the embassy, during the bus ride to the airport, on the tarmac, in the air, or on their way to the absorption center in Israel.

On one of the flights, a woman named Libe Mammo called for help. She was about to give birth. Dr. Dani Bezalel of Hadassah hospital came to her. He covered the area with a white *shammas*. At the moment when Bezalel checked Libe, she gave birth to two healthy girls. She named the first girl Israela.

The Israeli air force was equipped with medical equipment to deal with emergencies, and all the immigrants arrived safely.

PART THREE

THE LAND OF MILK AND HONEY

THIRTY-TWO

AFTERMATH

I watched the last plane disappear in the sky—with Kasa aboard! We had given him the green light to go to Israel. But we had a problem. How could such a known man as Kasa pass the emigration officers at the airport? His mere appearance might cause a commotion.

Eli Eliezri of JDC had a plan. He instructed his deputy Ami Bergman to bring one last sick person on a stretcher to the plane. Bergman had already brought several sick Beta Israel from Menelik and Yeketic hospitals to the airport; the emigration officers had stopped checking the people on the stretchers in his Toyota van.

Early Saturday morning, Bergman went to Kasa's house. The van was loaded with ten crates, doubtless filled with Kasa's valuables. There was just enough room in the middle for the stretcher. At 9:30 A.M., Bergman stopped at a stationery shop in Bole center.

Kasa slipped into the van and was immediately laid on the stretcher. Bergman covered him with blankets from head to toe. With the excitement Bergman drove fast through the potholes. Since the Toyota was rather old and the springs ungreased, Kasa was bouncing around in the back like a Mexican jumping bean, crying "Aye! Aye!" "Wow! Wow!" "Drive carefully!" and "Oy! Oy!" This was not the Mercedes ride he was used to.

On every bump, Bergman said he thought—*That's* for giving us problems with the visas! *That's* for sending back application forms! *That's* for blackmailing us!

At the airport, Bergman opened the back door. The guards didn't even bother to look and let the van pass. The van approached the plane, a Hercules, backward to its opened hatch. The cartons were unloaded and in the midst of the commotion, Kasa was led up the gangway and into the hold. Five minutes later, the Hercules took off for Israel. Just like Mengistu, Kasa left Addis like a thief in the night.

From the airport I went to the Hilton where the Greek ambassador was holding his National Day reception. When I entered, people clamored around me, wanting to know what had happened.

After I told them the whole story, Tadesse, the director of the Bank of Addis, stepped forward. "It's amazing," he said, "how much effort and money you are willing to spend to save your people. Tell me, Mr. Ambassador: How can I become Jewish?"

I didn't answer him. It was a rhetorical question. But I was full of emotion. It is rare that being Jewish could be considered providential. We Jews have suffered for more than two thousand years, always a minority and never a majority, stripped of equal rights, always having to fend for ourselves. The redemption of

Jews has been a command throughout history: *Im en ani li mi li, veim lo achshav eimatai*—If I am not for myself who is for me, and if not now, then when?

FRONT-PAGE ARTICLES around the world called the operation "a miracle." "Israel does it again," they declared. In Tel Aviv, homes and hotels alike were thrown open to the Beta Israel, clothes and food heaped at their feet. For hundreds of years, Africans have been taken from their continent in chains to be sold as slaves—on that day, for the first time in history, Africans were delivered from bondage to freedom as a lost tribe returning home.

I rested most of the rest of the weekend. Monday night, I made calls to my colleagues, in particular Angeletti, who always had better information than the rest of us.

Even he was in the dark. The radio news reported in brief bland nothings about the opening of the peace conference. These were the days before the Internet and satellites—when communications went down in a place like Ethiopia, you were truly in the dark.

Early on Tuesday morning, I was violently awakened by a tremendous barrage of artillery from cannon and tanks. The shots were from west to east, originating at a place that must have been very close to the Hilton.

I soon determined that the shots were directed at the presidential palace located three hundred yards south of the hotel. All the shots passed, whistling, over the Hilton's roof. Some shells fell on top of us, rocking the building and causing damage, but there were no casualties. David asked me to move into his room, which had windows facing inside the building, while the window of my suite faced the street.

There was a scary atmosphere, but no panic. David prepared coffee and cookies. The bombardment continued. David said they were signaling the Ethiopian units what to expect if the units resisted the rebel forces in their bid to take control of Addis.

When the bombardments were thick, David asked me to lie under the bed. I refused. We heard voices of the rebels outside. They sounded very close. We telephoned the Ministry for Foreign Affairs in Jerusalem. They were extremely concerned. The minister asked me to have a round-the-clock open telephone and continuous reports. I felt that I had to quiet them. They were more excited than we were! But I did ask them not to tell Hilda what was happening.

The first shelling went on for about forty minutes and then abruptly stopped. A few minutes later, David stepped onto the terrace to assess the damage. The minute he opened the door, a heavy smell of burned gasoline came into the room, and we saw a big fire rising up in the direction of the presidential palace.

David turned and looked at me mischievously. "By the way, Mr. Ambassador, shrapnel hit your car, which is parked under your window. A rather large piece has crushed your trunk." He wanted to drive home the message that he'd been right to insist on taking me to his room.

The silence was broken again with another barrage of shots, mainly from tanks. This onslaught was much less intense than the first one. The shells seemed to be coming from the Organization of African Unity buildings. There were four tanks lined on the street about thirty yards from our rooms.

THE HILTON IS situated between the presidential palace and the OAU buildings, which is why we ended up in the midst of the battle for Addis. When the shooting was over, David went out again and returned, saying that there were four more rebel tanks on the street in front of us, and that a car was driving around, announcing a curfew for the next forty-eight hours.

Again David—who had become like Noah's dove, checking the level of the flood—left and came back to report that the rebels had entered the Hilton and wanted the hotel guest list. Perhaps they thought that high-ranking Ethiopians from the government, business, or the military were hiding there?

I returned to my suite, which made David unhappy. It was just getting light. I found that the sliding glass doors to the terrace were open, and the tips of two bayonets were passing across them. Then I saw that two children of about fourteen carried the bayonets. They wore ragtag clothes, and each held an antique World War II rifle.

When they noticed me, I gave a big smile and clapped my hands in greeting. They looked at me without responding. I used my Ethiopian words for friendship: *"Endamin adderu,"* good morning.

They softened their grim faces and answered, *"Exaver immasgen"*—God bless.

I immediately went to the kitchen and offered them cookies. They contemplated whether to take them. The one with the sandals (maybe the hungrier of the pair) took the cookies and put them in his pocket. Then one took courage and put a cookie in his mouth. The atmosphere eased.

A few minutes later another child of maybe twelve approached, but to my utter surprise it was a girl. I ran for the cookies again and handed her some while greeting her with *"Exaver immasgen."* She smiled and took them. I was sure they didn't get cookies in their units.

David did not approve of my behavior with the rebels. "They are unknowns. We don't know how they react toward foreigners."

But he couldn't resist the temptation to chat with them in his proficient Amharic.

"These are the rebels that defeated the largest and best-equipped army in Africa?" I told David. "Look at them. Children with antique rifles, eating cookies."

THIRTY-THREE

KICKBACK

The London peace conference opened Monday, May 27, 1991. On Tuesday, rebel forces rolled over Mengistu's ten-thousand-commando unit at the presidential palace and took Addis. That left the rebels to negotiate among themselves on how to run the country. There was no sense doing that in London; they moved the conference to Addis.

In Addis, the rebels had their hands full trying to control the flow of tens of thousands of defeated government soldiers—penniless, hungry, in disarray, but armed! These soldiers could easily turn into a mob, wreak havoc on the country, and destabilize the fledgling government. Rebel units rounded up government, military, and political leaders and put them in a detention camp to stand trial.

Mengistu's acting president, Tesfaye Gebre Kidan, and other ministers got wind of these round-ups. Kidan's request for asylum at the U.S. embassy was refused, so he slipped into the Italian embassy and asked for asylum. He was accompanied by Birhanu Abayeh, former foreign minister Addis Tedla, and Hailu Yemenu—all members of the politburo.

Assuming (as they claimed) that they were in danger of being executed by the rebel regime, Angeletti had no choice but to agree to let them stay "as guests" (he refused to grant them asylum, which might have strained his relations with the new regime). Hailu Yemenu committed suicide with a pistol soon after he entered the Italian embassy—he was sure the Italians would hand him over to the rebels.

The remainder of the group refused Ethiopian court summons to appear before the judge, saying they didn't recognize the new regime and its court. So they were put on trial in absentia (together with forty-one other imprisoned Mengistu high officials). The court proceedings have been going on since then against all forty-five defendants with no end in sight.

The Ethiopian government has asked the Italians to hand this trio over to "stand trial for crimes committed against the Ethiopian people." The Italians have demanded assurance they will not be put to death. The Ethiopian government says it can't guarantee that because it is up to the court. This stalemate is ongoing.

The Italians are holding these officials in "prison conditions": They share the same house in the Italian compound. They are allowed out for only one hour, twice a day, and then they are only allowed to circle the house. They have Ethiopian food three times a day. They are allowed no visitors of any kind (in that sense they are worse off than in an Ethiopian prison, which allows visits by relatives). They are being guarded by Italian carabinieri (similar to police). Ethiopian soldiers are stationed outside the embassy to ensure they don't escape. This is the longest asylum that I know of in history, and the story isn't finished yet.

• • •

DAVID AND I inspected our embassy and found it safe and sound. Our Ethiopian guard told us the rebels had come, registered the embassy, and promised to protect it. We were relieved. Many dwellings had been invaded, including three embassies: Zimbabwe, North Korea, and Cuba—the countries that had been Mengistu's staunchest supporters.

During the next weeks, the embassy was quiet. The thirteen *tukuls*, which had been the center of activity for four thousand students, were deserted. A few Beta Israel who had fallen through the cracks of Operation Solomon would show up to seek help.

Emigration was at a standstill while the new government formed. But Zimna, who had flown back to Addis, and a JDC representative registered them and made sure they had medical attention, a place to live, and enough to eat.

It was not a sweet victory for the rebels. They inherited a devastated country, a shattered economy, hundreds of thousands of unemployed soldiers, and an empty treasury.

They had political problems as well. Asias Afaworki, the Eritrean leader, wanted complete secession from Ethiopia. Meles Zenawi, the leader of the Ethiopian rebels, acquiesced, apparently as part of an earlier Meles-Asias coalition agreement to unite to depose Mengistu. The United States interceded, and Asias agreed to postpone the referendum on secession for two years, to help Meles establish stability in the land.

But Asias behaved as a leader of a separate state from day one. He demanded that Ethiopians have entry visas coming into Eritrea. He disarmed the tens of thousands of Ethiopian soldiers at the Asmara-Keren enclave, led them to the border, and ordered them to march into Ethiopia through the scalding lowlands.

Many died of starvation and thirst. (Eritrea became formally independent two years later.)

MELES MADE IT clear that he would install democracy and a free economy. The statue of Lenin near the Hilton came down to cheers.

On June 1, Mesfin Sayoum, acting foreign minister, called a meeting of all foreign ambassadors.

"Our government will respect all international agreements and ensure your safety," he said.

"Let us forget the past and your relations with Mengistu," he told me. "We want Israel as a friend." I was relieved. But then he asked for the extradition of "the criminal Kasa" to stand trial in Addis.

As it turned out, he wouldn't relent on Kasa for the next two months, and I would begin to wonder if they would detain me in Addis until we delivered him. Why Kasa? Prime Minister Tesfaye Dinka and Foreign Minister Tadesse had asylum in the United States. There was no pressure, according to Houdek, to extradite them. And Zimbabwe had refused to extradite Mengistu, the real criminal.

Sayoum admitted there was no evidence that Kasa had committed crimes. But, he said, Kasa was the brains behind Mengistu. It galled me that Kasa could still cause me trouble even when he wasn't around. The day after my initial exchange with Sayoum, Israel flew Kasa to Switzerland so we could claim that he wasn't under our jurisdiction.

I WAS CURIOUS about the kickback Kasa had received for Operation Solomon. He had tried to extract two hundred dollars for every immigrant from Peter Jackson. I would learn that Kasa had been paid two million dollars by American Jewish groups for his part in the Beta Israel's release. I was outraged to hear that.

The thirty-five million dollars was released by the State Department, and I pressed for it to be spent to develop an irrigation system to stop Ethiopia's cycle of famine, plant twenty-five thousand hectares of cotton in Awash to serve as a basis for a textile industry, and establish a training center for nurses.

Sayoum told me that the cabinet had expressed its appreciation for the Israeli ambassador's concern for the Ethiopian people; unfortunately, the money was needed "for immediate use." That was one of my saddest days in Addis—an opportunity lost!

MEANWHILE HILDA RETURNED to Addis in mid-June, when the country had stabilized. We planned to leave our assignment as soon as two objectives were achieved: good relations with the new government and renewing the flow to Israel of Falashas who remained in Ethiopia.

The summer dragged on, but I had yet to meet with Meles on resuming the flow of Beta Israel emigration. He professed to have lifted the travel restrictions imposed on Ethiopians by Mengistu's government. The ministry of interior, however, was overwhelmed, and the emigration department was in shambles. Lines for passports stretched around the block. Not one Beta Israel had been able to obtain a visa.

Finally, I met with him on September 4, at the same palace in which Mengistu had had his office. The fearsome Mrs. Sheune was gone, replaced by a tall man in a blue suit with a cigarette dangling from his lips. He led me straight into that same hall with the same furniture that I had seen in my meetings with Mengistu.

Meles, in his midthirties, wore a simple gray suit. He spoke

English and got right to the point. "My people say Israel plans to convert tens of thousand of Ethiopians, whom you call the Falashmura, in order to bring them to Israel. Please inform your government that we consider this as interference in Ethiopia's internal affairs."

I was surprised, to say the least. "The Falashmura are not considered Jews by Israeli law, and my embassy isn't dealing with them. As a matter of fact, I never put this issue on the agenda."

Meles looked at his aides. "Why was I misinformed?" he said.

I knew why, but I didn't say anything. The Falashmura issue was (and is) being promoted mainly by the North American Conference on Ethiopian Jews (NACEJ), an organization that some Israelis accuse of being motivated by a desire to perpetuate its own existence. Its sister organization, the American Association for Ethiopian Jews, had dismantled after Operation Solomon. NACEJ, however, had received political support in Israel from right-of-center religious groups, who want Jews—any Jews—to settle in the West Bank and Gaza Strip. Some Israelis were upset that Barbara Gordon, the American woman who ran NACEJ, was deciding who was a Jew, instead of the Israeli government and the Knesset. "Why doesn't she bring these Falashmura to America?" they asked.

I immediately continued with Meles: "Mr. Prime Minister, I came here to talk about the fate of the four thousand Beta Israel in Qwara near the Sudanese border."

Meles interrupted: "We have no control in Qwara. The EPRP is a radical group that seems to be in love with revolution per se."

"My sources say that it is only a matter of time before the area will be under Ethiopian government control."

"True."

"For now, I want to resolve immigration for the five hundred

Beta Israel, stranded in Addis and Gondar, who, for one reason or another, missed Operation Solomon. These people need to unite with their families in Israel. Their stay here helps no one, but is harmful to their well-being."

"Ethiopia is now a free democratic country, like Sweden or Holland," said Meles. "Every citizen, Falashas included, has the right to leave at will. But we can't make special arrangements. It would not be fair. Let the Falashas stand on line with everybody else."

"Mr. Prime Minister, they have stood in line since June 1 and not a single Beta Israel has succeeded to get a passport to leave. If a Swede wishes to travel, he applies for a passport in the morning and flies that afternoon."

Meles looked for an explanation from his aides, but they kept quiet. "Three months is really too long to wait," he finally said. "We will have to allow some special arrangement. But no special operation or chartered flights. They leave in small numbers, twenty to thirty at a time, on scheduled Ethiopia Airlines flights. And please, no publicity."

On September 14, the first group of twenty-six Beta Israel emigrants flew from Addis to Israel via Rome. They made headlines in Israel and a big headache for me in Addis with Sayoum, who planned to suspend the special arrangement.

THE REASON FOR the publicity was the arrival of Tsega Melako's parents, who had missed Operation Solomon. Tsega, in her midtwenties, was an opinionated and ambitious young lady, the Israel-radio programmer in Amharic, a show that was broadcast daily for the Beta Israel. When Tsega (who came to Israel with Operation Moses) covered Operation Solomon for Israel-radio, she couldn't find her parents. She checked the airport arrivals, the absorption centers, and announced on her radio program, "If anybody has seen the Melako family, please call me."

Soon the whole country knew of her worries. The prime minister's office in Jerusalem called me in Addis to determine the whereabouts of her parents. It turned out that when they had been called for the operation, they had rushed to the market to sell their belongings. By the time they were through, the operation was over. Zimna arranged for them to leave with the first flight on September 14, and their arrival became a media event.

I would soon become friends with Tsega and learn her history. She had grown up in Gondar and emigrated to Israel on her own in 1984. She studied accounting and enrolled at Bar Ilan University. There she met an Ethiopian student her age, fell in love, and married him without consulting her parents—something unheard of in the traditional Ethiopia of arranged marriages. Moreover, she had married someone who was only five generations distant, instead of the required seven.

"At first I thought they would never forgive me," she would say to me. "But, you know, we Ethiopians are a very emotional people. When they finally landed in Israel and saw me we all started crying, and I knew that all was forgiven."

THIRTY-FOUR

RESOLUTION 3374

I left Addis on September 21. Emigration had been renewed. There were no outstanding issues with the Ethiopian government. My eleven months in Addis had been full of action from day one. Routine had begun to creep into my work, and I was ready to go.

On my return to Israel, Foreign Minister David Levy honored me as the Distinguished Civil Servant of the Year. So did Prime Minister Yitzhak Shamir at a special ceremony in the Knesset. Ultimately, President Chaim Herzog bestowed on me the Distinguished Civil Servant Award for the whole country for 1991.

Frankly, I was embarrassed with this attention. I felt I had done what had come naturally. In simple words, I did my job!

Hilda and I knew that our involvement with the Beta Israel wasn't over. Saving the lost tribe and bringing them home to Israel had been, perhaps, a miracle of a sort. But we knew that the bigger miracle would be to turn the community into contributing citizens of the state. In a four-hour flight, the Ethiopian immigrants had moved from a barter to a dotcom society.

Prime Minister Yitzhak Shamir congratulated me in his office for a job well done. "We have done a great *mitzvah* in gathering this lost tribe into Israel. What shall we do next?"

"Mr. Prime Minister," I replied, "if we have a dollar, spend ninety-nine cents on educating the young. They are the future. They are intelligent. Some are bright, and all are eager to learn. Education is the key for a better future for them and for Israel."

HILDA RENEWED CONTACT with Yehudit. We visited her and Rivka at Givat Hammatos, the absorption center in south Jerusalem. Yehudit wanted to move as quickly as possible into an apartment of her own.

Israel grants Ethiopian immigrants many more benefits for housing than it does to any other immigrant group. The government pays up to 90 percent of the mortgage cost, and covers the remaining 10 percent in a thirty-year mortgage at a very low rate. This policy is meant to encourage independence. Owning property comes with responsibility of taking care of it and gives the Beta Israel the feeling of having a home.

Rivka, Yehudit's daughter, was learning her first Hebrew words: *ani rotsa* (I want), and *ani lo rotsa* (I don't want). Rivka was Yehudit's whole life. And in that first visit, Yehudit was already talking to us about her education, a process in which we would become intimately involved.

WE WOULD HAVE continued to explore how the Falashas were making out in Israel, but in October Reuven Merhav called me:

"Pack again," he said. "We have nominated you as a member of Israel's UN delegation in New York. Your rank is ambassador and you will serve on the UN committee that deals with racism, racial discrimination, and self-determination. The Falashas' story will serve us well in our campaign to erase the hideous UN resolution equating Zionism with racism."

In my first appearance before the committee, I addressed the Arab chairman. I told him of the persecution that I had experienced as a boy growing up in Tripoli, Libya, contrasting it to the color-blind policy of the Zionist state of Israel, which received the black Ethiopian Jews as equals.

"I can trace my family tree to the third century in Libya," I said, "three hundred years before Islam. When I was a child growing up, I lived in a mixed community of Jews, Muslims, and Italians. Arab children threw stones at us on our way to school. Why? Because we were Jews. After World War II, the Allies conquered Libya. Arab nationalists opposed the British occupation. So what did they do? They burned Jewish shops and houses, even though the Jews were not involved. Why? Because the British forces were stronger than the Libyan militants, while the Jews were weaker and an easy target. No one came to our defense.

"I have just returned from a tour of duty as Israel's ambassador to Ethiopia—a wonderful country with talented people. I was involved in a historic event called Operation Solomon, the emigration of 14,200 black Ethiopian Jews to Israel. For centuries, black Africans had been taken from the continent in shackles on slave ships. Now, for the first time in African history, black Africans left Africa for freedom. In Israel, they were received as a lost tribe that had returned home.

"Therefore, Mr. Chairman, UN Resolution 3374 that equates Zionism with racism is a lie, preposterous and unjustified, and I call on it to be repealed for the sake of the United Nations' honor, and for truth and justice."

The Arab delegates were furious, particularly the Libyan ambassador. "Ambassador Naim can return to Tripoli at any time," he said. (Where I should expect what? Kaddafi's prison? Even the Arab delegates laughed.)

A vote of 111 countries for and 25 against repealed Resolution 3374. It was the first—and the only—UN resolution ever to be repealed.

THIRTY-FIVE

KUSHI

After four months in New York, we returned to Jerusalem, ready to till our very nice garden and settle in, but I was called on to reopen the Israeli embassy in Seoul, the Republic of South Korea. At sixty-two, it was my last posting. I liked the challenge of a new embassy in a new environment; a new embassy is like a blank canvas to an artist, open to creation.

In Korea, I initiated agreements on aviation, trade, and cultural exchange. Trade between Israel and Korea more than quadrupled, from $158 million to $712 million, during my tenure. I also arranged the first visit of an Israeli prime minister, Yitzhak Rabin, to Korea.

"This is it, Hilda," I said as the tour was ending. "Retirement. Relaxation. No more traveling around. Back to our home and garden."

She looked at me and indulgently smiled. "Who do you think you're kidding, Asher."

• • •

WHEN WE RETURNED to Jerusalem in the summer of 1995, we renewed our friendship with Yehudit and Rivka. That was when we became friends with Tsega. Zimna visited us when he was back in Israel. He was still working with the Jewish Agency in Addis and Gondar to help the Beta Israel who remained in Ethiopia emigrate.

Qwara had, indeed, come under government control, and the Beta Israel were brought from there to Gondar, where they were housed until all their paperwork was ready for their flight. Then they were brought to Addis and put directly on planes. Although AIDS was rampant in Gondar, it was easier to control them in the small provincial capital than it had been in the sprawling chaos of Addis.

The Qwara Jews had had a rough time. The rebel group that had controlled the region had said they would be slaughtered if they tried to leave. Or, if one family member left, the whole family would be put to death. To complicate matters, some Beta Israel had given testimony that the Qwara villages weren't really Jewish.

We sent in people to investigate. They went on foot—a trek of three weeks. They determined that indeed the Qwara population was Jewish, and it later came out that testimony to the contrary had been spurred by a long-standing conflict between two groups of *kessim*. Like Jews everywhere, it turned out that the Beta Israel had its own *mishegoss*.

MICAH ODENHEIMER, WHO had covered events in Ethiopia as a correspondent for the *Jerusalem Post*, was the person who had led this investigation into the Qwara Jews. Like so many of us, he had become engaged with the Beta Israel through his professional life and ended up devoting himself to their plight.

In June 1996, he called me in Jerusalem and told me he had formed the Israel Association for Ethiopian Jews (IAEJ). Odenheimer introduced me to Uri Tamiat, IAEJ's executive director, the first Beta Israel to be appointed to such a high executive position.

Uri, in his midtwenties, was a big chunky guy with a round face and the beginnings of a paunch. He was capable and talented. He had spent several years in kibbutz Ma'ayan-Zvi in Beth Shan valley, married a kibbutz-born woman, and had a daughter with her. In 1994, he had left the kibbutz and entered public life.

We hit it off from the start. Micah and Uri introduced me to the IAEJ board members, all non-Ethiopians.

"Most Ethiopian Israelis are under eighteen," said Micah. "We have a tremendous opportunity to help this new generation, who will be as Israeli as anyone else. But this isn't being done! We need government programs for tutoring, free books, and computers to help Falasha kids with their academic studies."

Uri nodded. "We want to increase the number of Ethiopians at the university from 8 percent today to the national average of 38 percent in ten years," he said. "I don't know if you're aware, but a significant number of young Ethiopians are in trouble. We would like to show you what could happen if we don't act quickly."

THEY ARRANGED FOR me to visit the IAEJ club in the central bus station in the old section of Tel Aviv, the city's slum, where foreign workers find places to sleep. The neighborhood is flooded with seedy clubs, cheap restaurants, and bars. An eight-story concrete building houses the station. Inside are all kinds of shops, little restaurants, and a steady flow of travelers.

Uri walked me around the neighborhood before we went into the station itself. Reggae and rap poured from some of the clubs.

"This is a haunt for young Beta Israel," he said. "These kids feel alienated, misunderstood, and rejected. They are seeking their identity in the black music of Jamaica and America. They escape from the boarding schools in which many of them have been placed. They get lost in this terrible place, and they resort to stealing, drugs, alcohol, and prostitution."

"What are these boarding schools?" I asked.

"The government thought that they were a way to give the Beta Israel a quick education. But most of Israel's boarding schools are designed to educate children with family and behavioral problems, so Ethiopian high school kids found themselves in the company of less-than-desirable Israeli role models. In dormitories, the Ethiopians turned clannish. They were bullied and called *kushi* by kids at school or by ignorant people in their neighborhoods. You know what *kushi* means."

"No."

"Nigger."

When he said this, my blood ran cold.

We entered the station itself and walked along a maze of sloping walkways to an upstairs room with no windows. It was comfortably furnished, and against one wall was a kitchenette. This was the club.

"We make it known to all Ethiopian youth that we are here to help," said Uri. "We don't impose ourselves. They come to eat, talk, or even find a place to sleep. They don't have to steal or prostitute themselves to get their basic needs met. A social worker is available to help talk over things that bother them."

Two Ethiopian girls in their late teens entered. They wore black leather pants, high heels, and short-sleeved black shirts. Their hair was tinted blond. I couldn't believe my eyes—they had transformed from the Ethiopian girls whom I had met in Addis. They seemed to have lost their innocence.

"*Tannestellin,*" I said in Amharic. They seemed puzzled and curious.

"Where are you from in Israel?" I asked. They laughed, the same bashful laugh I knew so well from my Ethiopian sojourn, and cast down their eyes. The change in appearance might be superficial, I thought—not a change in their essential character.

Yossi, an Ethiopian in his early twenties who ran the club, pulled me aside. "They won't answer you," he said. "First, you have to gain their trust. That takes time."

We strolled out into the hall. It was all commotion, people racing to and fro, the busy shops. "Let me tell you about these two girls," Yossi said. "Their parents live in Afula, a northern city. The shorter one, Sarah, has an old stepfather who imposed on her the old Ethiopian tradition of housekeeping and total obedience. She says that he sexually abused her, something rare in Ethiopian society. A social worker placed her in a boarding school near Haifa. She complained to the staff there that other children called her '*kushi.*' Her teacher punished the name callers. Then the other students ostracized her for 'spying.' Her friend brought her to the bus station, and she has fallen in with Russian mafia types. She has worked as a prostitute and been involved with drugs, all in just six months! We are encouraging her to come to us as often as possible and offering her different alternatives with the help of the social worker. You can't push too much or work too fast. But we have made good progress with Sarah. If we succeed with Sarah, we believe her friend will follow."

BACK AT THE club, an Israeli woman soldier arrived and invited Sarah and her friend for a drink.

"What is the soldier doing here?" I asked.

"The army allocates women soldiers to help work with troubled kids," said Uri. "They serve as role models. We are now looking for Ethiopian women soldiers to help us. Hopefully, we'll find some soon."

Eight Ethiopian teenagers came into the club.

"How many kids come here each month?" I asked.

"Perhaps a hundred," said Uri. "We don't keep lists. All our work is discreet. They know that. That is why we are successful."

Uri was very anxious to get me involved. "Every one we save is worth all our efforts," he said. "In Israel, education is key. We lobby the government and American Jewish institutions to create special programs to fit the needs of Ethiopian immigrants and a special system of intensive education for Ethiopian children."

"ASHER, WHAT'S WRONG?" Hilda asked me when I got home that night.

I told her about my experience.

"That's terrible," she said. "What can we do?"

"I don't know yet, Hilda," I said. "But I know we have to do something."

BLOOD TIES

G od may have promised the ingathering of the tribes, but how they are absorbed into Israel depends on what we do on earth. If the bus station phenomenon expanded, we could create a black ghetto in Israel similar to the ghettos of inner-city America. I know about these ghettos and their problems, having served as Israel's consul general in Philadelphia from 1976 to 1981.

I was haunted by Rivka's singing "Jerusalem, Jerusalem" on my first day at the embassy in Addis and the feeling I had had during Operation Solomon when I saw the planes take off. I felt the work that I had done was in jeopardy.

YEHUDIT CAME CRYING to our house one day soon after my trip to the bus station. A scandal was ripping through the Ethiopian community. The Beta Israel had patriotically donated large quantities of blood to Magen David Adom (our Red Cross). But the Ministry of Health secretly dumped the Beta Israel blood because Ethiopians had a high AIDS rate.

During Operation Solomon, the AIDS rate among the Beta Israel had been 1 percent, the virus largely contracted through Beta Israel men frequenting prostitutes in Addis. The rate rose to 8 percent after Operation Solomon, since many of the immigrants had spent a longer time in Addis than their predecessors.

In January 1996, Ronael Fisher, a reporter for the Maariv newspaper, published an article revealing that all blood donations of Ethiopians had been secretly dumped. The Beta Israel deeply resented that the government had acted behind their backs. The act seemed to further marginalize people who felt themselves struggling against great difficulty to become part of mainstream Israeli society.

Tens of thousands of black faces converged on Jerusalem from all over the country. OUR BLOOD IS LIKE YOURS read the posters they carried as they demonstrated in front of the Knesset and the prime minister's office. During the demonstration, some of the crowd exploded in violence, hitting policemen, knocking down barricades—totally unlike this quiet, gentle people. Perhaps they had learned such tactics from us.

The president apologized to the Beta Israel and declared that Ethiopian blood shouldn't have been secretly dumped, but he didn't recommend rescinding the directive not to accept blood donations for use from the community.

IT ALWAYS AMAZED me how much Yehudit knew about current events and gossip about different Ethiopians. "We talk on the phones," she said in her slow, quiet way. "Of course, in our villages in Ethiopia we had to make do without them," and she laughed.

I told Yehudit about my trip to the bus station.

"I'm glad you went," she said. "Many of us are going through drastic change and hardship."

"But you seem to make ends meet. Aren't you happy with Rivka's progress?"

"I don't mean me."

"Are you saying people want to return to Ethiopia?"

"No, no, no! Some Ethiopians are going back for business or tourism. We are grateful to have come to Israel. But many of us have had difficulties with the absorption process, particularly the older generation."

Yehudit was looking down at the tablecloth and bunching it in little folds between her forefinger and thumb. She hadn't touched the plate of cookies I had set before her.

"I can tell something is still troubling you, Yehudit. What is it?"

She gave a heavy sigh and shifted in her seat.

"It's the Russians," she finally said. "They came when we came. There are so many more of them—eight hundred thousand—and the Israeli public is so excited to welcome them—all the doctors, scientists, professors, computer programmers, and musicians. Once Operation Solomon was over, the Israeli public directed their attention to the Russian Jews. We know they have strengthened the Jewish majority in Israel, and contributed greatly to the Israeli Defense Forces. But still, it hurts to be overlooked and be seen as disease carriers who can't do much to contribute."

"Yehudit," I said, "don't play one group against another. The Russian Jews were also persecuted. They were denied visas.

Almost all the Jews who have gathered in Israel were, at one time or another, singled out. Remember, we are all one people."

"I know, Asher. But I think that it's hard for us to feel that way sometimes."

TSEGA ALSO BECAME a frequent visitor at our house. The foundation for my relationship with her had been laid when I helped find her parents in Addis and made sure they got out on the first plane after emigration had resumed. She contacted us when she heard through Yehudit that we were back in Israel. Hilda had been tutoring Yehudit with her English, and Tsega asked Hilda to help her with her English for her exam for a master's in business administration. Soon, she felt like family.

I was always impressed with Tsega's strong character and straight talk. Soon after the blood-dumping debacle, she visited us.

"I am not impressed with the Beta Israel demonstrations on the blood issue," she said. "People put health as first priority. Who wants to play Russian roulette when he needs a blood transfusion?"

Hilda and I were surprised that she didn't automatically side with the Beta Israel, regardless of the issue. I sensed there might be a schism opening between Ethiopian men and women. After all, it was the men who were infecting the women and were the primary carriers of the disease. This was on top of the tension between the sexes in Israel that was already rife.

Tsega had been dealing with a clear case of these tensions. Her husband, Wasihun, was an engineer and worked for a high-tech company. Tsega's fast promotion at her job in radio and television programming in Amharic for the Ethiopian community didn't sit well with Wasihun's traditional concept of a wife's place in the family. There was also a bit of envy. Tsega was more successful than he was.

Strong-minded Tsega wanted no one to stand in the way of her career—including her husband. She said that the rise of independent Ethiopian women in Israel had caused family problems and some divorces. And she talked about the disparity between men and women in the Beta Israel community.

"There are now more than a thousand Ethiopian students in university," she said. "And the majority of them are women. They advance in Israeli society faster than men. We women seem better able to adapt."

"Why is that, Tsega?"

She looked me straight in eye. "We are just better than they are," she said.

"Come on, Tsega."

"It's true."

TSEGA HAD BEEN investigating a story on the complex situation with the Falashmura—Jewish converts to Christianity—who had been immigrating to Israel by the thousands with the support of right-wing religious groups.

"The Falashmura converted because they wanted to enjoy the benefit that comes with being Christian in a Christian country—education, ownership of land, and government jobs," she said. "They attended missionary schools, which were the only schools in most parts of Ethiopia. That is the reason the majority of Beta Israel are illiterate. But now that Jews are being redeemed by Israel, it suddenly pays to be Jewish. The Falashmura want to return to the faith and are willing to reconvert, even in the most rigid orthodox way. The entire state of Gojam, in northern Ethiopia, six million people, is asking to be recognized as Jews! How will Israel deal with this demand?"

"How do you think? The government is in accord with the Ethiopian activists and the North American Conference on Ethiopian Jews. We have recognized twenty-five thousand Falashmura who are eligible for *aliyah*. That's it. I don't care how hard the right-wing groups will push to increase Israel's Jewish majority. The Gojam request will have no support."

I KNEW THAT I wanted to somehow help the Beta Israel, but Uri's group did not feel quite right for me. They were involved in social work, and that was not something I wanted to do. Around this time I met the Nobel Prize–winning author Elie Wiesel and his wife, Marion, in New York, who told me about Beth Zippora, an after-school enrichment program that their family had established in Kiriat Malachi in southern Israel for Ethiopian children.

Hilda and I visited Beth Zippora. The children learned English, arithmetic, and how to use computers. The students were diligent, eager for knowledge, and intelligent. I learned that the Jewish Agency, Education Ministry, JDC, and New Israel Fund—among others—were doing similar programs with kids of different ages. That restored my confidence that Israel was trying to help the Ethiopian community, and that the episodes at the Tel Aviv bus station were the exception not the rule.

Zimna and others stressed that the most important thing for Ethiopian Jews was to create Ethiopian leaders. "We want Ethiopian doctors," said Zimna, "Ethiopian engineers, Ethiopian teachers, and, yes, Ethiopian generals!"

• • •

I WANTED TO help educate the Beta Israel, but I wasn't sure how until I met Sarah Anyor, the wife of Ambassador Hanan Aynor, a veteran Israeli diplomat, who had served before me as the Israeli ambassador to Ethiopia. Like the rest of us, he and Sarah had developed a special attachment to Ethiopia and the Beta Israel.

After Hanan's death, Sarah had established the Keren Hanan Aynor Foundation, whose purpose was to grant university scholarships to Ethiopian Israelis. I knew as soon as I heard about it that this was what I was looking for. Five retired Israeli diplomats comprised the board: Reuven Merhav, Avraham Cohen, Arieh Oded, Benad Avita and me. Micha Feldman and Tsega were also on the board. We were all volunteers.

Benad noticed we weren't giving out scholarships for science. So we approached an Israeli philanthropist (he prefers to remain anonymous) who financed a program to educate Ethiopian students through high school in math, physics, chemistry, English, and computer science. The idea was to develop a cadre of Ethiopian Israeli scientists.

The program was successful and began to draw large numbers of applicants. More funding was necessary, so I decided to open a foundation branch in the United States. Sidney Haifetz, a businessman and philanthropist from Philadelphia, helped me set up The Scholarship Fund for Ethiopian Jews.

Our manifesto reads as follows: ". . . we are in danger of allowing the many Ethiopian Israelis to fall into a cycle of impoverishment, bitterness, and despair. . . . The Israeli government has been generous in investing funds to facilitate Ethiopian absorption, more than its expenditure per capita for any other immigrant group. Nevertheless, a sizable portion of the immigrant population is failing to bridge the culture gap between the land of their birth and the modern society that they have encountered in

Israel. . . . The community is without Western-educated leadership that can represent the needs of the community to the Israeli establishment, provide guidance, and serve as role models for leading successful lives. The elders of the community, in particular, are victims of the culture gap. They cannot serve as models of self-sufficiency. As a result, they are unable to prepare the younger generation for modern life. Together we can prevent the creation of underclass in Israel."

I MET THE *Kes* of *Kes* once more. He was very old at this point. His son was there, who had trained to be a rabbi. What a sight: the *kes* in his white robes with his turban and his whisk and his son standing next to him in the black coat and tall black hat of an Orthodox rabbi. Rabbi Hadana translated for us.

"You made it to the Holy Land," I said to the *kes*.

"Yes. Here I am! Now I am ready to die."

"Remember once you told me that perhaps one day you would introduce me to a Jewish monk?"

"I remember."

"Can I meet him?"

The *kes* and his son conferred. It seemed only one Nazarene had made it to Israel, *Kes* Beyenne Demose. Hadana said he had just died in Ashdod. "He refused to touch any other person," Hadana said, "for cleanliness rules. He wouldn't even shake my hand!"

"Would he touch your father, the *Kes* of *Kes?*"

Hadana translated and the *kes* laughed, shaking his head.

"No. Not even my father," Hadana said.

In Gondar, the Nazarene had lived in a cubicle, so small and with such a low ceiling that he couldn't even stand up straight. He prayed all the time. He had a bump on his forehead that was caused by his constant prostrations, touching his forehead to the packed dirt floor of his tiny room.

"In Addis and later in Israel he learned to extend his hand covered with his *shammas*," said Hadana.

"That was smart," I said.

In Israel, apparently, the Nazarene lived in a neglected shelter, near a synagogue in Ashdod. His diet consisted of fresh vegetables, dried peas, and water. He prayed most of the day and lived like a hermit.

"So there are no more Jewish monks," I said.

"No," said the *kes*. "The last monk died in Israel."

THIRTY-SEVEN

ZION

W e bundled into the car, Uri in front with me, Yehudit in back. The sky was clear and blue, a cool, bright fall day. We drove southeast through the city, skirting the German Quarter, rising up out of the Hinnon valley.

The traffic, as always, was murderous. All Israelis drive like maniacs, me included. What can I do—it's a habit. Everyone is aggressive and impatient. We don't like to follow the rules. We cut each other off and smash our horns.

We parked at the Peace Park, in the southeastern part of the city. We walked up the road, groves of cypress and cedar to either side, the air sweet with their scent. It was just before noon, and already thousands had gathered. As far as I could see, mine was the only white face.

We left Yehudit, and Uri took me up to join the elders. The procession started and they carried the Orit, balanced on top of their heads. We moved toward the lip of a hill that looked north over Jerusalem.

"Shalom!" said Uri to Rabbi Hadana in his black coat and hat. Uri leaned forward and kissed Hadana quickly three times on alternating cheeks.

Jerusalem spread before us. New housing projects sprawled over barren hills. At the Western Wall, Jews *davined* in long black coats and black hats. At this distance, they were tiny black specks. On the road to the village of Abu Tor, an Arab in a red-and-white *kaffiyeh* rode sideways on an ass. He swiveled slightly, flicked his switch, and the ass quickened. I stumbled on loose rocks. Uri reached out a hand to steady me. The sound of the city drifted upward: traffic, bells, prayers. Across the steep scoop of the Kidron valley was the Mount of Olives and the Garden of Gethsemane.

Uri was not happy. "This is our tradition, but out of eighty thousand only a few thousand come. The young people want to assimilate." He pointed to their ballooning pants and T-shirts with images of American rap stars. "They all want to be Puff Daddy."

I had to laugh. "Seriously, Uri. This is a good turnout!"

"These rituals, this tradition—it is our unique contribution. Our form of Judaism. And we're losing it."

Tsega joined us. "Face it, Uri," she said in her quick, incisive way, "we lived in primitive conditions in Gondar. No running water, toilets, refrigerators, or electricity! And our traditions were primitive. Never updated. We had stood still!"

Uri lapsed into silence. I looked across the Judean hills into the West Bank, toward Jericho and Hebron. During the riots that fall, Yossi Tabjeh, an Ethiopian officer in the Israeli border police, had been killed not far from here at Qalqilyah by a

Palestinian police officer with whom he was in a joint patrol to keep the peace. The Palestinian had shot Yossi at point-blank range, yelling, "Allah is great." The Ethiopian community mourned him, and we had set up a special scholarship in Yossi's name.

THE *KESSIM* WALKED ahead, marked by their squat white turbans. Rabbi Hadana wasn't with them. Yehudit had told me there had been complaints in the Ethiopian community that he had not done enough, that he had been too flexible, too soft, too accommodating to the rabbis—that he had not stood up for the Beta Israel traditions. There was money involved, of course. Government funding that goes to build and staff the synagogues and schools that some members of the Ethiopian community would like to see teach Amharic and the indigenous Ethiopian religious traditions, as well as the Israeli style of Judaism.

Uri was right—the Beta Israel's traditions were changing. I sensed among them a shyness I had not encountered at this same holiday ten years earlier in Ethiopia. Their eyes dodged mine. They were unsure of how the old ways fit into their new life. A woman knocked earphones from her son's head. Uri flinched. A Walkman on a sacred march?

The *kessim* were in full form, deep in a holy trance. They sang out prayers and *davined* in deep bows, fingers brushing the ground, with a sweep of their robes.

We arrived at the hill's edge, and the Orit was opened at last. The women ululated, a wild heckling cry, a thousand birds taking flight. Then *kessim* began singing from the books of Ezra and Nehemiah, where the wandering through Sinai is recalled. Uri translated for me:

You, so greatly loving,
Still did not forsake them in the wilderness:
The pillar of cloud did not leave them
That led them on their path by day
Nor the pillar of fire by night
To light the way ahead of them

The whole ceremony was song, with many calls and responses from the elders, a highly charged and intensely melodic recitation. I quickly fell under its spell.

"It doesn't feel right here," said Uri. "Where is our sacred mountain? The highest, purest spot. We are too close to cemeteries and buildings. What is this modern clothing? Where is the cotton of home? Only on the elders—where it will remain until it is buried with them."

"One day, Uri, you'll see. Maybe not this generation, but the next will come back. All will not be lost. They will make a great contribution to our society, to Israel."

"*Halvai!*"—I wish.

"None of us would trade the life here for the life in Ethiopia," Tsega said. "Isn't it true, Uri? On this can we agree?"

It surprised me when he slammed his fist into his open hand. He said, "*Betah nachon!*"—Sure true—without a moment's hesitation.

Then he was lost to us. He closed his eyes and tilted his head back, his face to the clear blue sky, his skin glistening. The *kessim* chants carried over the hilltop. The wild cries of the women echoed over the hills to Bethlehem and Jericho. I felt the ancient prayers filling my soul, cool water, brimming over, making me whole. The prophecies were not just words. For two thousand years we had been waiting for this moment, and it had arrived.

263

The last tribe had come home. Some of the old people wept, moved in the presence of the old ways, perhaps remembering their former lives, celebrating the *Seged* as children with their parents long ago on the sacred mountaintop outside Ambover. Or perhaps they were moved to be here, in the land of our fathers. The wind blew over the Temple Mount. Bending his knees, Uri started singing the prayers.

ACKNOWLEDGMENTS

T his story derives from my personal experience serving as Israel's ambassador to Ethiopia. Some of the material was gathered from people I encountered. Other material came from reading and interviews that I conducted while I was in Ethiopia, and after I left. It took more than ten years to trim, combine, edit, and bring my experience into a concise, readable book.

I am grateful to many friends and colleagues from the Foreign Ministry who have encouraged me throughout the ten years with reference material and constructive guidance, in particular Ambassadors Avi Granot, Eytan Bentsur, Moshe Yegar, Yehuda Avner, Director General Reuven Merhav, and the late ambassador Hanan Aynor. They wanted to see this story told.

Most of all I would like to thank Peekamoose Productions and Kenneth Wapner, my very talented collaborator, who skillfully assisted me in writing this book. He has been a tower of strength and support. Through the collaboration we have become friends. Kenneth introduced me to Gail Ross, my dynamic agent from Washington, who believed in this project and found me Tracy Brown, my editor at Ballantine Books. Tracy's trust and direction helped bring this book to an early printing.

Acknowledgments

Special thanks goes to Professor Efraim Isaac, director of the Institute of Semitic Studies at Princeton University, for his important remarks, encouragement, and constructive contribution in personally reviewing all the material several times and joining me twice in Ethiopia. I wish to thank Professor Steve Kaplan, head of African studies at Hebrew University in Jerusalem, and Professor Hagai Erlich, head of African studies at Tel Aviv University, for their contribution.

I owe many thanks to Dr. Eli Schwartz and Dr. Rick Hodes, two most prominent specialists in tropical diseases. I thank Amnon Mantver, Micha Feldman, Avi Mizrahi, Ami Bergman, and Pamela Loval in Israel, and Sidney Haifetz, Robert Houdek, and Rudy Boschwitz in the United States. For their valuable assistance, I wish to thank my Ethiopian-Israeli friends—*Kes* Hadana for his graciousness in giving me his version of the origin of Beta Israel, Rabbi Yoseph Hadana for endless meetings and discussions on Beta Israel tradition and custom, Uri Tamiat, Yehudit and her daughter Rivka Reuven, Tsega Melako, Ester Ayub, Mamo Woodne, and many others both in Israel and in Ethiopia. And to Zimna Berhane, my friend, who has been key in the Beta Israel's exodus, I owe much gratitude and a very special thanks.

But above all I want to thank my wife, Hilda, for putting up with me through all these years in preparing this book. Her patience gave me comfort, and her encouragement gave me strength.

ABOUT THE AUTHOR

ASHER NAIM, an eminent Israeli diplomat, has served as the cultural attaché to Japan and the U.S. and the Israeli ambassador to the United Nations, Finland, South Korea, and Ethiopia. As the founder of the Ethiopian Scholarship Fund for Ethiopian Jews, Naim raises money for young Ethiopians living in Israel who wish to attend college and graduate school.